2001: A POETRY ODYSSEY LINCOLNSHIRE

Edited by Lucy Jeacock

First published in Great Britain in 2001 by
YOUNG WRITERS
Remus House,
Coltsfoot Drive,
Peterborough, PE2 9JX
Telephone (01733) 890066

HB ISBN 0 75433 038 9
SB ISBN 0 75433 039 7

FOREWORD

Young Writers was established in 1991 with the aim to promote creative writing in children, to make reading and writing poetry fun.

This year the 2001: A Poetry Odyssey competition again proved to be a tremendous success with over 50,000 entries received nationwide.

The amount of hard work and effort put into each entry impressed us all, and is reflective of the teaching skills in schools today.

The task of selecting poems for publication was a difficult one but nevertheless, an enjoyable experience. We hope you are as pleased with the final selection in *2001: A Poetry Odyssey Lincolnshire* as we are.

CONTENTS

Heidi Ward	70
Christopher Birchall	71
Robin Wilson	71
Helen Mackinder	72
Rahman Fuad	72
William Alcock	73
Paul Thomas	73
Emily Ward	74
Selina Hall	74
Catherine Griggs	75
Errol Dunham	75
Rachael Palmer	76
Rachel Walsh	76
Kim Beeken	77
Carl Newell	78
Leanne Kennedy	78

Lincoln Christ's Hospital School

Claire Jackson	79
Holly Nam	80
Calum English	80
Georgina Pearson	81
Clair Beaton	82
Lisa Dodsworth	82
Stacey Calvert	83
Victoria Hill	83
Edward Datta	84
Matthew Williams	85
Adam Johnson	86
Patrick Duce	87
Joanne Kingswood	88
Annabel Brewer	88
Tara Wheeler	89
Claire Langford	90
Kevin Trigg	91
Tom Jeyes	91
Vahini Sangarapillai	92
Gregory Boyfield	93

Kirsty Blakey	94
Gregory Powis	94
Rosie Cole	95
Emma Seward	95
Alasdair Robinson	96

St Hugh's CE School

Carly Haddock	96
Stacey Goodge	97
Terri-Anne Foster	97
Tammy Eldred	97
Mark Ward	98

Skegness Grammar School

Jennifer Cain	98
Tom Barton	99
Charlotte Bradbury	100
Samantha Oakley	100
Lizzie Schofield	101
Rebecca Johnson	102
Laura Geaghan	102
Sophie Bray	103
Callum Vine	104
Helen Jones	104
David James Hill	105
David Smith	105
Emily Rose	106
Ben Newman	106
Anne-Marie Quincey	107
William Forster	107
Leah Gray	108
Viki Bartlett	108
James Housam	109
Kerry Rogers	110
Camille Butt	111
Ben Amis	112
James Glenn	112
Joseph Hippey	113

The Priory, Lincoln School of Science & Technology

The Poems

HAVE YOU EVER BEEN TO REVERSETON?

Have you ever been to Reverseton?
Where the trees grow upside down
The people sting the wasps
And a verb is a noun
People live in water,
And they swim in the air
Their bodies are inside out
And no one has any hair
The sheep eat the people
And the grass eats the sheep
People have no mouths
So they can't even speak
There's no communication
So life's not very friendly
A year passes quickly
And a second passes slowly
You're born as an old person
And grow down till you're born
The day begins with dusk
And ends with dawn
People don't wear clothes
So they're completely stark naked
They eat their drink
And drink their food
When I was there ten years ago
I was completely shocked
So I had the gates of this weird town
Very securely blocked.

Jonathan Viccary (12)
Boston Grammar School

UNDERGROUND

The ground holds lots of wondrous things,
That have swum through water, and been carried by wings.
Here I list them, one by one.
The great and the horrid things they have done.
Submarines, bombs, swords and guns.
These are all murderous, terrible weapons.
Bones from dinosaur times, and before.
Creations of God, which man can explore.
Asteroids and meteors, rock from the moon and Mars,
Make meteorologists forget the stars.
Ancient countries, which fought and made peace,
Such as Egypt, Rome and Greece.
The ground contains pockets, such as caves and burrows,
House animals and people as cave painting shows.
As I conclude my poem on Earth,
I would like to say a word, as a new birth.
The ground is a crust, like orange peel,
Hiding the mantel and the core (all that is real).
It's like a person, for although the surface may change,
Inside it always stays the same.
So next time you feel technology pulling the world to pieces,
Remember
It's what's inside that makes humans the superior species.

Cal James (12)
Boston Grammar School

HARRY POTTER

T he story is as tense as ever
H arry is yet again in trouble
E veryone thinks Sirius Black is after Harry

P rofessor Dumbledore is helping out Harry
R on is worried about his pet rat scabbers
I gnorant Draco is tormenting Harry
S nape is again favouring Slytherin
O verjoyed is Malfoy when Harry is being stalked
N ow for a while Voldemort is out of the way
    Sirius Black is after Harry
E ven the lady is afraid of Sirius
R on doesn't know that his rat is a changeable human

O f all Harry's friends, Ron is his best
F irebolt is Harry's from a mystery person

A t Hogwarts the Dementors are causing havoc
Z ombie-like Dementors whose kiss make you worse than dead
K een are the Dementors to perform their deadly kiss
A bject Sirius is not actually after Harry
B almy Sirius is after a rat
A ccomplished wizard is Harry but he is no match for Sirius
N ow Sirius is caught, the Dementors are ready to perform.

Ben Carr (11)
Boston Grammar School

SEASONS

In the fields are flocks of lambs
Whilst the farmers are planting vegetable treats
Newborn are agraze in the fields
The time of year has come, as newborn are sprung upon us.
It's time for hard work for farmers, for harvesting the crops
School holidays, yippee for some and not for others.
It's that time of the year for getting a tan,
As people go abroad to venture the foreign land.

Autumn days when the grass is jewelled,
And the conkers falling from the trees.
All the leaves are piled upon the floor,
Whilst the people shop for Christmas treats.

Christmas trees are brightening up our houses.
As Santa's elves get working hard,
The postie's bag gets heavier and heavier,
As the children can't sleep on Christmas Eve.

Mark Bridges (11)
Boston Grammar School

CHESS

The battlefield is cloaked in darkness.
The board is flooded with lightning that illuminates the black
and white chequered squares.
In the eerie silence that follows there is the clank of armour.
The king turns to you, ready to order his servants to march to
their deaths.
A pawn draws his weapon impatient for the upcoming slaughter.
With a final flash of lightning, the king sighs, a knight moves forward
and the war begins . . .

Stephen Fendyke (12)
Boston Grammar School

THE LONELY GARGOYLE

The gruesome grizzly gargoyle had no friends.
His face was greasy and grimy.
His eyes were big and bold.
He had a big, black, slimy spot on his forehead.
He wanted a friend; he needed to be liked.
Why was he so ugly, so ugly, so horrid?
He thought he was the worst in the world.
He was sick of his looks and ways.
He felt like a human but looked like the Devil.
When he was alone he walked into a dark cave.
He heard someone sobbing, he drew closer and closer.
He saw something so repulsive
He didn't want to look.
It was another gargoyle, a replica of himself.
Two wretched gargoyles with spots and grease and grime.
But it didn't matter anymore
At least they were two of a kind.

Adam Cartwright (11)
Boston Grammar School

A SCARY CASTLE

Down the road on top of the hill,
A castle stood quiet and still,
There were bats in the belfry and rats in the hall,
And a grandfather clock that stood very tall,
The ivy climbing very high I could of sworn it touched the sky,
Just looking sent a shiver down my spine
I'm going home now I think it's about time.

Paul Jarvis (11)
Boston Grammar School

THE MYSTERIOUS OCEAN

Under the ocean is a world of its own,
Only a fraction of what goes on down there shall ever be known.
Shipwrecks hold mysteries, which only fish may tell,
Some say if you go near them, you can hear the fatal ringing of the
captain's bell.
Lives lost at sea, can never be counted,
Along with doomed ships which on the seabed are now mounted.
Coral reefs glitter, and fish are galore,
Seashells are so many you could never see more.
When I go snorkelling the world is in different motion,
I guess that's one of the secrets of the mysterious ocean.

Craig Hildred (12)
Boston Grammar School

A HOLIDAY POEM

Holidays, holidays lovely sunny holidays.
All the tasty food and all the barbecues.
The swimming pool's hot and cold.
Huge slides shooting down then *splash!*
Long nights out dancing and partying
Really late to bed, might not get to sleep.
Stay in bed all day without a care.
Lots of sightseeing and being amazed.
Also lots of swimming in the sea.
Making sandcastles all day long.
Lots of drinking in the bar.
Watching TV all night long.
Loads of playing arcade games.
Holidays, holidays all fun in the sun!

David Best (11)
Boston Grammar School

FUTURE CITY

Hey! Do you want to be free in your own town?
Do you want to climb up skyscrapers and bungee-jump down?
Do you fancy a holiday to the moon?
Vacancies are going, you'd better turn up soon!
Do you like beaches, trees full of peaches, and apples?
Oh! And don't forget penthouse blocks, small, tall, don't fall!
We've got it all, and all you need to do is call!
The countryside, the town, the corner shop, the mall,
A stadium for monster trucks, a stadium for football!

Come to Future City, everything is free,
It's a life of luxury, in a penthouse or up a tree!
We've got virtual reality games for the gaming freak in you,
Or if you're a wild thing, join the super bike crew!

If you like what you see, we'll give you the key,
Come and live in Future City, life's great here, believe me!

Dan Smith (12)
Boston Grammar School

FUTURERAMA

Get in a time machine
Go fifty years into the future
This is what I see
Flying cars here and there
Tigers by the dozen
Humans evolving with powers
But normal humans dominate
A comet will destroy Earth
As the rescue attempt fails
I get back in the time machine
And hope to change the future.

Sam Leafe (11)
Boston Grammar School

ZOO HOUSE

My brothers, the apes jump to and fro.

The doors moan and groan,
Like a lion with a toothache.

The toy cars roar past
Like cheetahs after prey.

Lights glare, the TV flashes,
The curtains draw back and forth,
Friends act like elephants.

Our tortoises roar past,
And knock everything flying.

The toilets gurgle and spin open and close
While the toilet paper rolls up and down,
Looking like a frog.

Meanwhile a bear takes up reading,
Why can't the rest be the same?

Jack Hornsby (11)
Boston Grammar School

RAINDROPS

Raindrops falling everywhere,
On the rooftops and in the roads.
In the gutter water swirling,
Pouring down a nearby drain.

Pitter-patter on the pavement,
Pitter-patter on the grass.
Soaking anything and everything,
In the raindrops' path.

Headlights glistening through the rain,
Windscreen wipers wiping,
Bits of litter plastered to the ground,
People hurrying by.

The sun comes through,
And raindrops fade.
Wipers off, headlights off,
No more rain today!

Thomas Atkins (12)
Boston Grammar School

JERRY

I'm very small,
I'm brown and white,
Very soft like cotton wool,
I live in a cage with a house and a wheel,
My name is Jerry what am I?

I nibble on nuts and have lots of treats,
My family like to play during the day,
I like to play at night, not in the day,
My name is Jerry what am I?

I like to hide in the dark at night,
And run on my wheel to my delight,
I like to act like an acrobat,
Swinging on the bars of my cage,
My name is Jerry what am I?

I am a hamster,
Small and brown.

Adam Metssitane (11)
Boston Grammar School

HE WAS THERE NO MORE

I walked into the room,
It was silent and still.

He was there no more.

I looked at the chair where he sat,
Beside where his drink used to stand.

He was there no more.

There was no life, movement or sound,
I was alone.

He was there no more.

The room felt empty,
There was something missing.

He was there no more.

I knew he was gone,
But he was there.

He was in my heart.

Nathan Talbot (12)
Boston Grammar School

WINTER

W inter nights sat round the fire
I   n the house telling stories
N   orth wind blowing outside
T   ree branches crashing down to the ground
E   ach passing day the wind grows stronger
R   ustling leaves flutter to the floor.

Adam Brackenbury (11)
Boston Grammar School

MY VIEW OF THE FUTURE

In the future the world will have changed a lot,
People won't do housework but will have robots.

They will have cars that are solar powered,
That will reach speeds not fit for a coward.

They will have teleporting machines,
So they don't need to use their legs again.

Planes will run on fizzy pop,
And carry 4000 people top.

People will be able to live on the moon,
They will get a space bus there at noon.

Man United will have done the treble,
While other teams are in for trouble,
Because Boston United are second best
And Arsenal have fallen lower than the rest.

There will be a new species of dinosaur,
That will live away so far and far!

Liam Mundt (11)
Boston Grammar School

THE FUTURE

F   stands for flying skateboards,
U   stands for Uranus holidays,
T   stands for technology,
U   stands for unidentified flying object,
R   stands for robots that do the housework,
E   stands for elected aliens for a government.

Tom Ruck (11)
Boston Grammar School

DISNEYLAND, FLORIDA

D isneyland is the best place for a holiday
I   magination comes alive
S ee all your favourite Disney characters
N ever-never land is a great ride
E pcot is the future waiting to be explored
Y ou can see smiles on everyone's faces
L et your imagination run wild
A nimal kingdom is the best place if you're an animal lover
N ever see sad faces
D ifferent rides waiting to be explored

F lorida is a great destination
L isten to the ocean's roar
O rlando is a city in Florida
R ain hardly visits the place
I   'm feeling hot, hot, hot
D esert beaches to be explored
A merica is great.

Leon Pycock (11)
Boston Grammar School

HITLER'S WAR

People dying, bombs are flying
German planes are dispersing
Soldiers killing, trainers willing
People shooting, blood is spilling
Markets ration, love and passion
English soldiers gonna bash 'em
Hitler's ruling, English losing
For the German 'twas amusing.

Thomas Ogilvie (12)
Boston Grammar School

HOMER J SIMPSON

Simpson is his name
Eating is his game
Cannot stand his boss
His money is at loss
Snuggling with Marge his wife
Is the best thing in his life

Flanders makes the steam come from his ears
Despite living next to him for ten years
Homer's dad's a lean mean talking machine
But towards him Homer's all mean

Daughter Lisa plays the sax
And naughty Bart is the Mad Max
Maggie likes her red dummy
To Homer pork chops and donuts, yummy!

But for Homer wherever he chooses to go
Life is a laugh and a *d'oh!*

Neil Achary (12)
Boston Grammar School

SMITH POEM

S   melly,
M   en in brown coats are after him,
I   rresponsible,
T   hieving is how he lived his life,
H   iding something from everyone.

Leon Kita (13)
Boston Grammar School

A LIFE AT SEA

The winds whistle
The seas roar
The waves splash
Feeling sick after a meal of hard tack
And meat soup, which turns your stomach
And your smile into a frown.
I yearn for a hot fire, smiling family
That I will never see again.
And the excitement of being part of the life at sea
And all because:

The winds whistle
The seas roar and the waves splash.

Robin Jeffreys (12)
Boston Grammar School

MY IMAGINARY FRIEND

His name is Zann,
And normally arrives with a very big bang.
He wears a yellow shirt,
It is covered with dirt.
He has a banana as an ear,
And can barely hear.
Some bright green trousers,
And parties in other people's houses,
He may be weird,
But he's not feared.
He's my imaginary friend,
With a cool new trend.

Ben Porter (13)
Boston Grammar School

AN UNWELCOMED GUEST

The house howled in the wind,
I was afraid, but I had to go in,
The huge door creaked open,
I was only just coping,
I went up the stairs,
And I saw some grizzly bears!
I went into a room,
And there I saw my *doom!*
A wormhole sucked me into a cellar,
When I got there I found a propeller.
I tied it to a piece of wood,
Should I go home? Yes, I should.

Ben Lees (11)
Boston Grammar School

A SCARY HOUSE

I open the door, it creaks so loud,
I walk in and see a passing shroud,
The door slams shut behind me,
The cobwebs go in my eyes so I can't see,
The stairs squeak and creak,
My heart pounds as I feel weak,
Suddenly a hand blocked my way as I got to the top,
I ran down before, it could make me stop,
The eerie noises hurt my ears,
I grappled with the door amidst my fears.

I got out and ran and ran and ran.

Douglas Lee (11)
Boston Grammar School

MY VIEW OF THE FUTURE

I saw a floating house
Some flying people and a mouse.
A spaceship came from nowhere
Through the window I spotted our mayor,
The spaceship landed close to me
So I thought it was best to flee.
Next to the bright, shiny yellow stars
Were some red flying sports cars,
Higher still I saw an aeroplane
Underneath was a high speed train,
I thought, 'Oh no, they're going to collide.'
Luckily the train went up a playground slide
A lion was running around
I thought it was going to pound,
Onto the helpless deer
That just lay there in fear.
I said my goodbyes,
And then shut my eyes,
Pressed the button, to zoom myself home
Back where I come from, the Millennium Dome.

James Waters (11)
Boston Grammar School

THE CREEPY CASTLE

There is a castle,
Under the shade of trees,
Full of cobwebs
And lots of leaves.

The old castle stood
In the middle of the wood,
The towers were tall and high
Stretched up to the moonlit sky.

The old grey stones were cold
And overgrown with mould,
The wind blew to make a sound
Which could be heard from all around.

Stuart Smith (11)
Boston Grammar School

THE GHOSTLY CASTLE

In the ghostly castle
There was never-ending hastle
There was undead bodies and bats
And the cellars were full of vicious rats

There is a howling in the mountains
I went to the window and closed the curtain
All the lights had blacked out
There was a blood-curdling shout

The shape of a zombie walked towards me
Now my pants were full of wee
I run to a room it was an armoury
I grabbed the sword that was the end of that zombie

I ran down 200 steps
I went right down to the castle depths
There was a horrible smell of blood
Now I felt I would spew up

I ran out of the entrance into the boundaries
Then I saw ghost ship in the seas
I ran all the way home to my mum
I told her all about it - she said that I was dumb!

Gareth Ranshaw (11)
Boston Grammar School

A GHASTLY POEM

Walking around the castle,
It is plain to see
And orchard winding all around
Where werewolves are supposed to be.

This place is so creepy
Send shivers down your spine
The place no one would go to
Unless they're out of their mind.

Old and derelict, all dull and grey,
Clothed in moss which creepy vines do lay
Appearing cold and eerie
It's always more scary towards the end of day

Supernatural spirits, a fear of the unknown
Live inside the tower
In which they freely roam
To them this is their home.

Aaron Robinson (11)
Boston Grammar School

THE GHOUL

The gruesome ghoul, the grisly ghoul,
Without the slightest noise
Waits patiently beside the school
To feast on girls and boys.

He cracks their bones and snaps their backs
And squeezes out their lungs
He chews their thumbs like candy snacks
And pulls apart their tongues.

He slices their stomachs and bites their hearts
And tears their flesh into shreds
He swallows their toes like toasted tarts
And gobbles down their heads.

Andrew Dawson (12)
Boston Grammar School

THE TRAIN JOURNEY

On board the train and here we go
In the stations they to and fro
Holbeach and Spalding and Boston too
From Leeds to Birmingham and Waterloo
The train blasts out a deafening whooo!

In the countryside, we are right now
Passing a sheep and a black and white cow
Whizzing past the green hills and trees
Open a window and feel the cool breeze
But in the winter it is sure to freeze

Travelling through the cold, grey city
It's such a mess it really is a pity
Smell the disgustedly polluted air
Passing shops that are selling rotten pears
Life in this dump is really harsh and unfair

Soon we will be getting off the train
Never again will our lives be the same
Finally we've reached our destination
The train's pulled in at the local station
We've all had a wonderful vacation.

Scott Relton (12)
Boston Grammar School

THE SPOOKY DOOR

Walking along the dusty road,
Searching near and far,
Looking for the door,
Never looking back,
Still looking for the door.

Poking my head left and right,
Pushing away vines,
Kicking away leaves,
Always looking for that door.

Owls going 'tu-whit, tu-whoo',
Dogs howling in the night,
But it doesn't scare me,
Because I'm searching for the door.

At long last I see a light,
I wonder what it is,
Slowly I creep forward,
At last I find the door.

Slowly I reach out,
To turn the rusty handle of the door,
I turn the handle and go inside,
The spooky door slams behind me,
All that I can see is darkness.

Ben Newton (13)
Boston Grammar School

THE FRIGHTENING FUTURE

Humans are outcasts,
Cockroaches rule.
There's no need for homework,
Cos we don't go to school

We will be slaves,
And the roaches will order,
We work day and night,
To get past the border.

Cops are invisible,
You cannot see them,
You can't get away
Even from eating.

The roaches are evil,
They kill for fun.
We're always on the run
From the cockroaches'
Fun!

Someday we will win,
And stomp those bugs flat,
We'll take back the world,
That will be that!

Jonathan Birkhill-Robshaw (11)
Boston Grammar School

A SPOOKY POEM

Ivy creeps up over the house
Dead flowers creep over the flowerpots.

Big cobwebs in the smashed windows
The rotting house infested by spiders.

Massive trees block it from sunlight
The cottage eternally enshadowed.

Stone gargoyles crowd the dark roof
Where rotten slates fall and smash to the ground

In the wind the manky doors creak
An owl hoots or a wolf starts to howl.

And at the front of the cottage
Are a pair of rotten giant front gates.

They loudly bang and they echo
Into the cold, cold, freezing night air.

Ben Grunnell (11)
Boston Grammar School

THE GLOOMY CASTLE

In the gloomy castle
There were never ending corridors
The cellars were full of rats
There were dead bodies and bats.

There is a howling on the rooftop
An organ playing in the library
The lights had all blacked out
There was a terrible shout.

A shape of a human walked towards me
When it stopped it sounded like thunder
I thought it was a ghost
Could it be a ghost - what? How?

Benjamin Charlton (11)
Boston Grammar School

THE FUTURE

Flying cars
trains and buses

Wars in spaceships
no air

Human police
have guns

Robotic police
have lasers

No freedom
just domes

No taps
no water

No TV
no entertainment

No petrol
just rain

1000 years later
rubbish

Joshua Reed (11)
Boston Grammar School

MEN IN BROWN AND SMITH

M   urderers they are but nobody knows,
U   know, I know where the document goes!
R   ousing suspicion about the men in brown they must . . .
D   estroy him before they go down.
E   arning by murder, ready to shoot.
R   eady to stab - the noise is mute.
E   veryone who goes about shopping in town
R   ealises not, murderers are the men in brown.
S   mith is the only one who knows about this
    but he will not do anything for he's *scared stiff!*

Andrew Hammond (12)
Boston Grammar School

COMPUTERS

C   omputers, can we live without them?
O   rganising our daily lives,
M   emorizing and keeping everything safe,
P   laying games, creating enjoyment and fun,
U   nderstanding them is often a trial,
T   ry the internet, day or night,
E   veryone can have a go,
R   ich or poor, young or old,
S   imply the *future*, that's what computers are!

Daniel Welbourn (12)
Boston Grammar School

THE HAUNTED HOUSE

There stood a dark creepy house,
You couldn't even hear a mouse,
Inside a creepy atmosphere was appearing,
When I started hearing,
The squeaks of a door,
And the creaks of the floor.
We walked on slowly,
I looked down lowly,
Checking for clues.
We approached a door,
Then I saw,
A white old cat on the floor.

Jake Brooks (11)
Boston Grammar School

THE CASTLE

It was a dark wet and windy night,
I saw the huge castle it gave me a fright,
The rain was pouring down,
I thought I might drown.
The bats, bugs and frogs we all over the place,
I thought they were trying to kiss my face,
Up to the castle I went
To deliver a letter I had sent.

David Tetther (11)
Boston Grammar School

GHOST POEM

I saw some zombies coming towards me,
I only just noticed there was one behind me.

So I ran into another room,
I turned around and heard a boom.

'Oh no' I said, my stomach rumbling,
Through the window a monster jumped and started tumbling.

I saw the monster big and scary,
I hated it cause it was hairy.

I used my gun and gave it a pow,
And what the monster said was 'Ohwh.'

Rikki Chamberlain (11)
Boston Grammar School

THE HAUNTED HOUSE

The derelict house,
Stood on the hill top,
Tiles were missing,
The windows were flapping,
The door was slamming,
The wind was whistling,
Lightning was striking,
Bats filled the misty air,
Wolves howled in the full moon.

Lee Dickinson (11)
Boston Grammar School

WORLD WRESTLING FEDERATION

WWF is very extreme,
With wrestlers like Triple H, The Rock and Rikishi.
The sport just totally kicks ass,
When mad wrestlers go on the loose, like Al Snow and Tazz.

Rikishi is fat, about 500 pounds,
He's quite cool, having made his hair into strands.
Whenever he finishes a match he does a little dance,
But I believe he is very utterly pants.

The Rock is the current champ,
Beating every man that in his way stands.
He deserves to be in the WWF,
When the crowd see him, the noise will make you go deaf.

Too Cool is true, they are Too Cool,
They are short and call every wrestler a stupid fool.
Scotty Too Hotty does his move, the worm,
Which takes the audience totally by storm.

Al Snow is a madman on the loose,
He will act like anything, a cat, a dog, or even a goose.
When he picks wrestlers up, he really starts to throw 'em,
But, I'm afraid, this is the end of my WWF poem.

Adrian O'Callaghan (12)
Boston Grammar School

SMITH POEM

S   melly, never takes a bath
M   oney maker
I   lliterate
T   hieving's how he grew up
H   e is a pickpocket.

Darren Woods (12)
Boston Grammar School

VIVIAN'S GARDEN

The latticed house, blooming flowers
Sweet maidens in their colourful bowers.
Trees of fruit, and honey sweet,
In this garden did Vivian I meet.

For a while to my enchanted eyes
The bower was of paradise,
Until the enchantment did fall away,
The latticed roof was made of bones,
The maidens were hideous skulls.
The flowers sweet were wasps that stung.
The fruit was seething and rotten.

And in the bowl I had been about to drain.
Lay the germs of death, disease and pain.

I flung it down and with one bound.
I fled from that enchanted land,
Far, far away while in my ears
Rang Vivian's laugh.
Forever and ever, will I roam
Never, never will I come home.

Annie Wallace (11)
Boston High School

NEW SCHOOL

I thought my new school would be very scary.
I thought my teachers would be big and hairy;
When the bus dropped me off near the gate,
Oh, my gosh, I thought I was late,
And when I went into the hall,
I didn't know who to talk to at all.
When I met my teacher
She was nice.
I've got lots of work to do,
And I do it all,
And it doesn't drive me up the wall.

Amy Skinner (11)
Boston High School

AUTUMN

Yellow and orange,
Red and brown,
Autumn leaves laid on the ground,
All different shapes and sizes
This lovely season is full of surprises,
The trees stand tall, ugly and bare,
It may be true but the weather doesn't care,
The wind blows strong,
The sun beams down,
The leaves dry out,
And fall to the ground.

Nicola Dickson (12)
Boston High School

THE FLEAS

The fleas have come to invade the Earth
We can't get rid of them even using mirth!

They seemed to have just appeared everywhere in town
So I have an idea, something to do with a clown.

Whenever a flea was in my sight I would put it in the light
My lighted room, which is my fave, it will end our troublesome days.

In the room is a circus tent, I know this sounds rather bent
But I will train them every day and then everyone will be
happy and gay!

In the tent are trapeze to amuse my little fleas
They will learn and become great and everyone will be my mate.

A tiny red nose for a tiny clown who will jump up and down
Making all the humans laugh till they run out of gas!

The acrobat'll turn round and round making people dizzy
Till it lands straight on its back, and that's what'll make the
humans crack.

My little lighted room is full of fleas, so tiny you can just about see
Them doing their little tricks, and walking around with tiny
walking sticks!

The circus day has finally come; the people have come to see the fleas
They will do their little tricks and people will hopefully be pleased!

The circus is well and truly over, the people grumpily bend over
To pick up their bags and things, and then go home to the itching stings.

The circus went very well right until the very end
When the fleas escaped, they jumped around the bend

They ran as fast as they could, oh well it's good so they should!
Those pesky things have gone forever, I hope they don't come back
Never ever!

Victoria Shaw (12)
Boston High School

EMMA'S YEAR

J is for January, and the time of new year,
The dew fresh in February, when spring is here,
M is March, crocuses on the way,
Along comes April, fool for a day,
May brings the strawberries, they're lovely and sweet,
June brings the summer, with warm sunny heat,
July is the holidays, sun, sand and sea,
August, the beach, is the place to be,
September begins a new term once more,
October brings Hallowe'en, ghosts, ghouls and more,
November brings Bonfire Night, with fireworks alight,
December brings Christmas, with joy and delight.

Emma Beck (12)
Boston High School

CATS!

Cats!
Are the most,
Delicate,
Little things

They
Jump about,
Crawl,
Their feet
Are like springs.

Their
Coats are made
Of the most
Eye-catching
Colours.

But by far,
With
Treats and
Hugs,
My nan's
Cats are the
Only ones I
Smother!

Cats! Cats!
Those beautiful,
Cats!
Give them all a home,
Don't leave them on
Their own.

All those
People out there,
Cats need loving
Care!

So come along then
People,
Let them into
Your home.
Take care of them for
The rest of their lives,
They're no longer
Alone.

Emily Gurton (11)
Boston High School

WHEN I'M OLDER

When I'm older, I would like
To hand-glide, jet ski and go on a hike.
To waterski, absail, travel the Earth
Canoe, parachute and then windsurf.

When I'm older I would like
To run for England, catch a pike.
Go on a safari, appear on TV,
Go in a hot air balloon, just you and me.

When I'm older I would like
To go to China and build a dike.
To go and visit the Dome and the Eye,
Become a vet, make others laugh not cry.

I'd like to do this and that,
And on my back get a pat,
But it all can't just happen like that!

Emily Dawson (11)
Boston High School

MONEY

When you have a friend
And money to spend
You can go shopping together.
If your friend comes to play
Bank your money for a rainy day
And you will be rich forever.

Matthew Gilliver (17)
Broughton House College

FRUIT MACHINE

Putting money in the fruit machine,
Pressing all the buttons,
Seeing if you're going to win,
But then you realise you've lost.

So you put money in,
Again and again,
Keep trying to win but keep failing.

Putting your hand in your pocket,
Pulling money out by the minute,
Stuffing it in the slot.

Again and again you keep trying,
Then you put your hand in your pocket,
And feeling no money.
You turn around and walk out of the door,
And go home feeling guilty.

Helen French (14)
George Farmer Technology College

I DREAM OF ZOMBIES

I lay there in the cold
I see figures
which look old.
I feel lonely
I feel scared
and I haven't come prepared.
They move closer
these creatures
moving closer and closer.
They look like they are dead
I pull the covers over my head.
I can't bear to look
my eyes won't shut
all I can do is yell.

I awake
it's a dream
why did I scream?
These faces, these creatures
they are all so mean.
I can't sleep anymore
they might come back
but not for sure.
These gruesome thoughts
make me feel sick.
It was all a dream
I fell for their trick.
Never again will
I dream of zombies.

Lauren Porter (14)
George Farmer Technology College

RALLY

A desolate car stands alone, in the middle of a rural area,
Its driver's eyes, fixed, on the green lights,
Waiting, intensely.
A flash of green and he's away, with impossible acceleration.
A perfect start.
The pitch of the low, buzzing exhaust note grows,
Until the first corner.
The frantic hand of the driver grabs the quick-shift gear stick
And rams it forward.
As the rear of the car is thrust outwards
Colossal discs slow it.
The throttle is again applied
And fire licks at the passing rocks as the turbo lags.

A shaky navigator bellows directions,
Interrupted by gigantic jolts.
Suspension squeaks under the immense pressure.
A hairpin turn looms.
With flawless timing the handbrake is grasped and wheels lock up.
The sports steering wheel is spun in a frenzied lunacy,
180 degrees right then 360 degrees left,
All four wheels spin upon the exit.
The desperate driver now scrambles for a better position.
Stamping on the accelerator,
He screams across the finish line.
An agonising wait for the results now begins.

Jack Carfrae (14)
George Farmer Technology College

FISHING

It was a cold and frosty morning
I'd just pulled up the riverside and looked at the river
It was calm, just like the grass with the dew on it.
The anxiety was building up inside me, just to get fishing.

I took my equipment out of the car
And took it down the bank
I set up my rod, estimated where the weights should go.
I dug a hole in the mud for my box
Put my rod rest in the ground and cast.

I'd only been sitting there for five minutes
Before catching a fish.
After that I longed to catch a big tench or carp,
All the other competitors were drawing in all the fish
As I just sat there.
Suddenly I got a big bite
I struggled with the fish
For about ten minutes
I pulled it out,
The fish weighed ten pounds.

Time went by slowly and I hadn't caught a fish
After I said that I pulled out a big one
It weighed even heavier.
I picked the fish out of the water
The end of the match
2nd over all
A pleasing day.

Stuart Seaton (15)
George Farmer Technology College

CHRISTMAS DAY

You wake up at 6.30
Everyone is still asleep
You sneak a look in your stocking
Chocolate Santa . . . Writing set . . .
Yeah! A Discman!
Mum, you read my mind!
You hear a shuffling noise
Finally, it's your sister waking up.
As the rest of your family crawl out of bed
The excitement starts to rise
Everyone walks downstairs together
To see the pile of presents
There's even more than last year!
When all the gifts are unwrapped everyone calms down.
Your mum starts the turkey dinner
Your sister is upstairs dressing
Your brother is scoffing his selection pack
And Dad is on the PlayStation
Just another traditional Christmas Day!

Lucy Crane (15)
George Farmer Technology College

THE SPIRIT

The wolf appears out of the mist
Like a ghost, a spirit appearing
The grey of his coat keeps him hidden
Stained with the memories of past blood

He howls his tale for all to hear
From the ice-topped mountain peak.
He takes his power from the
Mystic, glowing moon.

The magic in his eyes,
The piercing dark stare,
He sees through the white storm
With the power of his shadowy soul.

As he disappears through the wall of ice
He walks into myth and legend
He treads softly
As he disappears.

Robert Mitchell (14)
George Farmer Technology College

AUTUMN

There are lots of colours in the autumn season
Yellow, red, orange, brown, green,
All the colours of the changing leaves,
They crackle and scrunch when you walk over them.
There's conkers, nuts and acorns,
Falling from the trees above, like rain.
It's cold in autumn and windy.
You don't see animals in autumn,
They all hibernate.
Most of the birds migrate, like swallows and geese.
There are hedgehogs and squirrels which all come out in autumn.
The squirrels come out on the damp and dewy mornings
Searching for their stock of acorns.
People walk down the roads in padded jackets keeping warm,
Treading on the scattered seeds
Which have been blown down the road by the wind.

George Beeken (14)
George Farmer Technology College

DANCE

Dance in the morning,
Dance at night,
Dance in the evening,
You can dance whenever you like.

Dance to the music,
Dance in your head,
Dance in your house
Or you can dance in your shed.

Most of all I like the dance machines in Skegness.

Dance, jazz, modern, pop,
Dance, rave, rap or rock
Try to dance and it will give you a shock!

Amy Smith (14)
George Farmer Technology College

SEASIDE

It comes nearer while it gets bigger,
Faster it goes as it roars,
Pushes everything in its path,
Spitting everywhere when it hits you,
Tickling you when it pushes past your toes.

Stepping back on the dry warm floor,
Sticking to you like a magnet,
Sinking slightly as you walk,
Rubbing your wet feet and making them sore.

You turn round as you walk away,
Waves crashing against the sand,
Thinking what a great day.

Gemma Courtman (14)
George Farmer Technology College

THE DEADLY EAGLE

He stands proud as he watches over his kingdom,
Then he spots dinner,
He springs into action to make the kill!

But as he does he's being hunted as well,
By the ferociously hungry wolf,
And boy does the eagle know he's being hunted!

So he has to decide between food or life,
He foolishly chooses food,
But I think the menu's changed to the wolf!

The eagle makes one sudden turn and dives on the unexpectant wolf,
But the wolf doesn't know it yet,
The eagle strikes with no mercy and once again is victorious!

Sam Dalrymple (12)
George Farmer Technology College

LIKE A SNAKE

It's as sly as a fox
Fast as an ox
Sharp as a sharp tooth
Cleverer than me and you

Slides along the ground
When you look he can't be found
Under the sand they hide away
Through holes and burrows to catch their prey

Most snakes use venom to kill their prey
If you're lucky you might get away
Python, rattle, grass and cobra and all snakes
So just go careful, no mistakes. *Sssssssss*

Sam Curson (11)
George Farmer Technology College

BIG BROTHER

July 14th began the blast,
Out of 10 which one will last.
Andrew, Sarda, Nicola and Tom,
They were all my number one.

Which one will last I thought each night,
It's going to be one hell of a fight.
Nasty Nick he did the deed,
Upon his paper it did read.

Vote for Craig he's the next one out,
I'm telling you there is no doubt.
Claire came in but was shortly gone,
Off she went back to where she came from.

Seventy thousand was the prize,
Now Craig's a star in England's eyes.
For 64 days we watched him live,
And all he did at the end was give.

I thought him obnoxious, whiny and crude,
In fact I thought him rather rude.
10 other people wanted the cash,
One by one their hopes were smashed.

Craig came out with a big gleam,
Telling us 'appearances are not what seem'.
He gave his winnings all to Jo,
To help pay for the op she needed so.

I really thought him rather dim,
But I'd rather have a friend like him.

Kellie Brogan (14)
George Farmer Technology College

BEST FRIENDS

Best friends are like good books,
You don't always like them
But when you need them
You know where to find them.

Best friends are like boyfriends,
You don't always love them
But when you need them
You know where to find them.

Best friends, you love them,
You care for them,
You don't always need them
But they know you care.

Best friends are like . . .
Nothing else but,
Best friends!

Tina Paske (14)
George Farmer Technology College

THE COAST

The coast is like the edge of the world
The line between the known and the unknown
The call of the seagull is a reminder of the hostility
Battered by gales for most of the year
The coast is a beaten space
The towering cliffs are no match for Mother Nature.

Liam Sisson (14)
George Farmer Technology College

GOALKEEPER

There I stand all alone
My knees trembling with nerves
My eyes in contact with the ball
All the bright flashing lights in the crowd
Distracts my attention.
I turn back
Oh no!
The ball is making its way towards me
Closer and closer
I can see all of the bright lights
Out of the corner of my twitching eye
The fine detail of the players
Coming into vision

There I wait in anticipation,
Getting more and more hyped up
For the consequences.
Gaining towards me, here it comes!
12 yard box,
He shoots,
The ball flies through the air
Like a coin
Tossing and turning
I reach up to grab it
It hits the crossbar
Rebounds out to their player

I moved out towards his position
The whistle blows
Cheers arise from the crowd
I look around

My buddies running around
Making fools of themselves
We had won!
The pressure was off.

William Tree (14)
George Farmer Technology College

DIRTY TO CLEAN

The car got dirty
Oh! Did I get shirty
Had to wash it clean
Now it's got a gleam

Housework was a chore
My mum found it a bore
I took the job in hand
Now I'm the best cleaner in the land

Dust made me sneeze
It brought me to my knees
Took my duster to get it away
At last hip hip hooray

Clean as a new pin
All rubbish in the bin
Neat and so trim
My house is never grim

Spick and span
I've done all I can
Everything is put away
Now I can go out to play.

Adam Blundell (11)
George Farmer Technology College

FOOTBALL

The ground starts to get full,
The fans start to glare down
The players looking around to the crowd
They know the specific task they have to do.

Everyone's hearts are racing dramatically
Scarves, flags and shirts supporting their wonderful clubs.

Goal they call him wizard
Then a frantic sudden moment in the match
Suspicious penalty
Some fans break down in tears.

The match is over,
Disgrace as the reds walk down the lonely long street home.
Emotional tears for blues cup final
Three weeks time 2-0 against the champs.
Now ready for next week's local derby brawl.

Matthew Black (14)
George Farmer Technology College

MILLENNIUM OLYMPICS

The glitter and glamour of the opening and closing ceremony.
The determination of the athletes to win a medal.
Every competitor has the burning desire to win gold.
Every sport needs great skill, from running to swimming and
                              even shooting.
Every athlete trains hard for four solid years to do their
                              countries proud.
The Millennium Olympics will go down in history as being very
                              memorable and a great Olympic Games.

Nick Franklin (13)
George Farmer Technology College

LAURA ALL ALONE

I walk past her day after day,
The stench of her travels through the wind,
I don't know if the stench is from her hair or her clothes,
But what I do know is that she needs a bath and new clothes.

Her name's Laura by the way,
I know that because I talk to her every day,
She never told me why or how she became homeless,
Sometimes I buy her something to eat and drink,
I also gave her a pillow and blanket once and some old clothes.

I think she enjoys my company,
I enjoy hers, she's very friendly,
I wonder if I'll see her tomorrow,
If she makes it through the night,
Through that bitter cold wind.
I hope I'll see her tomorrow.

Charlene Anderson (12)
George Farmer Technology College

MY HOMELESS NIGHTMARE

As I sit in shop doorways feeling cold and damp all over my body
I see people pass, looking at me as if I have done something wrong.
I am getting sadder and depressed as the days go by.
Ginger keeps me going by staying strong,
I put on a brave face but really I am breaking up inside.
I am getting dirty and smelly and I won't be able to survive
If I don't get a wash.
I am making a few coppers and when people
Say something it depresses me even more.

Andrew Warnes (12)
George Farmer Technology College

A White, Winter Snowfall

Classroom chairs, still and quiet
Nothing to do but hold you
Feeling like a chair.

Noisy teachers, loud and moody
Teaching you things that you don't like
Giving out detentions.

A heavy, winter snowfall
White as a sheet on the ground
Tiny snowflakes fall.

Then bursts of light through the clouds
Glittering on the white snow
Melting it slowly.

Tiny raindrops fall from the sky
Like someone's crying up above
Falling on everything.

Falling inside with soaking feet
Wet hair and clothes for everyone
Now it's the end of break.

Rachel Knott (11)
George Farmer Technology College

Football

Football a child's dream
Football a teenager's life
Football an adult's religion

Winning or losing
We will always be there
Watching or playing

Fighting for the points (or)
Flying high
Football is always fantastic

Weather doesn't matter
Weekend runabouts
We will always be there.

Carl Stamp (14)
George Farmer Technology College

PANDA POETRY

The icy-white, dark-black
Panda lurks about in the
Forest deep under.

Bamboo shoots is what
It eats, but I can see
He has a special treat for his tea
Birds and fish it will be.

He creeps along the
Grass at night,
Seeking out his prey
To *fright!*

His shimmering coat
Shines in the moon
Light!

The icy-white, dark-black
Panda lurks about in the
Forest deep under.

Jemma Gray (11)
George Farmer Technology College

SARAH PAYNE

Take this as a warning, dear parents,
Look after your children with care.
Always love, cherish your precious ones
And teach them with strangers beware.

What a start to the year,
It was a beautiful day.
On a visit to their nan's,
Four children went out to play.

One little girl ran off that day
And didn't come home the next,
Nor the next, nor the next;
Her mother was sorely vexed.

Search parties, police and volunteers
Scoured the fields and the dykes.
Could they possibly find a lock of blonde hair
From this poor little tyke?

Parents and family did not sleep a wink,
Waiting for the news by the phone
While constantly running through their heads
'Will she ever come back to her loving home'?

At last the phone rang:
'A body's been found,
Twelve miles from your home.
We need to identify, can you come down?'

The funeral started;
They let the white doves fly.
Tears trickled down their faces,
You couldn't help but cry.

The family didn't let go,
Demanded a change in the law.
So Sarah's Law was suggested
So paedophiles could do damage no more.

Holly Tointon (13)
George Farmer Technology College

PADDINGTON RAIL CRASH

At six minutes past eight the Western Express,
Was heading for Paddington Station,
A sickening crash heard miles away,
Was enough to rock the nation.

A great big fireball roared down the carriage,
Yellow, red, orange and black,
Never before was this disaster so great,
On this dangerous railway track.

Some emerged covered in soot,
Others lay injured or dead,
Covered in blood, oh what a sight,
Others sat holding their head.

The carriage all mangled,
It's a miracle that we were spared,
The police and ambulances are finally here,
Though alive, we were all shocked and scared.

An eerie silence fell over the scene,
As people were taken away,
People were crying, bewildered and shocked,
What a terrible start to a day.

Gemma Brinton (13)
George Farmer Technology College

JAMIE BULGER

Chorus:
Jamie Bulger at the age of three,
His mother's pride and joy,
Will never see his fourth birthday,
That poor young, Liverpool boy!

Three years and going into town,
Holding hands with his mum,
Wandering in and out of shops,
Two boys said, 'With us come.'

John Venables and Robert Thompson,
Both under the age of eleven,
Were the names of the killers
Who sent little Jamie to Heaven.

They took our little Jamie away
And at that track he cried;
With sticks and stones they broke his bones
Until little Jamie died.

The police and people looked everywhere;
They searched and combed the ground.
As the darkness of night slowly falls,
Jamie's battered body was found.

Parents and family got no sleep at all,
Waiting by the phone.
Thoughts were going through their heads,
Waiting for Jamie to come home.

We waited and waited for hours;
When at last the dreaded news came,
That filled us with sadness and sorrow,
Bitter grief, numbness and pain.

The world united in disbelief
That two so young could kill.
Angels now watching over Jamie,
His life cut short, and still.

Rebecca Hammond (13)
George Farmer Technology College

SYDNEY OLYMPICS 2000 100M SPRINT

One event.
Every four years.
One venue, on the other side of the world.
One of the fastest events every four years.

They walk up to the blocks already warmed up.
All cameras flash as they crouch down.
On your marks is shouted as it echoes round the stadium.
Bang! The starting gun fires its shot.

Like a flash the runners jump out of the blocks.
As the adrenaline rushes through their bodies.
It's a blur as they get faster.
The muscles pumping and rippling with strength.

The pink tarmac lays in front of them with one objective.
White lines divide each one of them.
The roaring crowd pushes them on.
The gold medal is in their sights.

They all cross the line together.
It's a photo finish.
Everyone goes quiet as they await the result.
And America has won, the crowd roars.

And all this happens in just 10 seconds!
Until the next four years.

Stephen Hansord (14)
George Farmer Technology College

A FRAGILE ENDING

As I looked down the scope on my rifle,
Sweeping the area with my rifle looking for a target,
A swift moving troop ran across my field of view,
He hid behind the barricade,
Placed there by our troops,
With a long stare down my scope
I saw him again,
He poked his head around the corner of the barricade,
I slowly squeezed the trigger,
The bullet hit him right between the eyes,
Within just moments of his body hitting the floor,
People ran to aid him,
How peculiar,
So I ran down the bell tower stairs,
I stood and glared with shock,
It was Private Jones,
A man from our own unit,
The men who aided him were my own troops,
I never forgave myself . . .
To this very day.

Ian Austin (15)
George Farmer Technology College

ON THE SEASHORE

Sand blows all around me
Up and down the beach it goes.
The sea is like a monster
Eating all the stones.

Children playing in the sand
Building sandcastles with their hands
The sun is shining on the sparkling sea
Fishermen set out in their boats for tea.

Pebbles shining on the seashore
Rockpools filling with sea
Slipping seaweed creeping crabs
People paddling, having a laugh.

Jemma Gray
George Farmer Technology College

JAMES BOND 007

James Bond 007
In the ladies' eyes they think he is 'heaven'
In his suit he carries a gun
Which is just for business, never for fun.

A drink of Martini shaken not stirred
And after, time spent with glamorous birds
He shoots all the bad guys - it's always a thrill
007 licensed to kill.

Q comes up with gadgets for Bond to use
Most of them have some kind of fuse
Bond races and crashes all of Q's cars
Anyone else would end up behind bars.

Did he really like Moneypenny, or was it a tease?
Or maybe he pretended just to please
In his immaculate suits he always looks good
But Moneypenny never knew quite where she stood.

He killed off Oddjob, Baron Samedi and Doctor No
That's three films down, sixteen to go
His name is James Bond 007
All the girls think he's 'heaven'.

Tim Cole (13)
George Farmer Technology College

BOY DAVID

He came from the country, Peru,
But he caught an awful disease.
His nose was eaten away,
So that he couldn't even sneeze.

David was a lovely young boy,
All he wanted to do was play.
Now he's famous throughout the world,
Looking forward to each dawning day.

When he was only three years old,
A lovely woman took him away with her.
They went across the ocean,
To see a powerful doctor.

David was a lovely young boy,
All he wanted to do was play.
Now he's famous throughout the world,
Looking forward to each dawning day.

They checked him up and down,
To see if he was okay.
They said that he was fine,
And to come back another day.

David was a lovely young boy,
All he wanted to do was play.
Now he's famous throughout the world,
Looking forward to each dawning day.

Finally, after a few years,
They made him a brand new face.
Day and night they would work,
To fill the empty-looking space.

David was a lovely young boy,
All he wanted to do was play.
Now he's famous throughout the world,
Looking forward to each dawning day.

Fortunately for him,
He got a new family too.
And now he doesn't feel left alone,
And doesn't feel so blue.

David was a lovely young boy,
All he wanted to do was play.
Now he's famous throughout the world,
Looking forward to each dawning day.

Now he's 25 years old,
And what a life he's had.
Seeing that little boy like that,
Had made us all feel sad.

David was a lovely young boy,
All he wanted to do was play.
Now he's famous throughout the world,
Looking forward to each dawning day.

Heather Rice (13)
George Farmer Technology College

SARAH PAYNE

Sarah Payne went out to play
In the wind and the rain,
But never knowing if she would
Ever see her loving family again.

> *Sarah was a sweet girl,*
> *Who was loved by everyone,*
> *But now they all miss her*
> *Because little Sarah's gone.*

They searched for her
All day, all night,
Never stopped looking
Until they got it right.

> *Sarah was a sweet girl,*
> *Who was loved by everyone,*
> *But now they all miss her*
> *Because little Sarah's gone.*

Her parents waited, worried,
As the nights drew thin,
They all sat crying, praying
For little Sarah to walk back in.

> *Sarah was a sweet girl,*
> *Who was loved by everyone,*
> *But now they all miss her*
> *Because little Sarah's gone.*

The police found frightening evidence
After searching for days.
They went to tell her family
As they sat, as they lay.

Sarah was a sweet girl,
Who was loved by everyone,
But now they all miss her
Because little Sarah's gone.

They finally found a body,
But was it hers, we had to know?
Her mum identified the body
And yes, it was hers - oh no!

Sarah was a sweet girl,
Who was loved by everyone,
But now they all miss her
Because little Sarah's gone.

Emma Fisher (13)
George Farmer Technology College

DODO

The dilly Dodo went into the town
The people there gave him a funny frown
All of the hunters there shot him down

The people who lived in Mauritius
Thought that he was really delicious
I suppose he was nutritious

Now since 1681
The hunters sing a sorry song
'Where have all the Dodo gone?'

James Pascoe (12)
George Farmer Technology College

THE RUNNER

Run, run, runner man,
As fast as you can
Faster than the speed of light,
Smoother than a bird in flight.

Run, run, runner man,
No one can catch the runner man,
Swifter than an arrow,
Out-running his own shadow.

Run, run, runner man,
Quicker than a rocket!
Into deep space, spinning a comet.

Run, run, runner man
Lighting the houses of the night.

Run, run, runner man,
Out of sight.
Run, run, runner man run!

Adam Bailey (13)
George Farmer Technology College

HELP ME WRITE A POEM

Help me write a poem,
I don't know what to write,
I'm not sure where I'm going
With this poem I need tonight.

I know I'm not making sense,
I never am able too,
It's leaving me in suspense
Of this poem I need to do.

Words are mounting on my page,
Coming bit by bit,
Maybe I'm at the stage
Where this poem could be it.

Kate Atkinson (14)
George Farmer Technology College

THE TIGER

He is 8ft long,
He's orange and black,
He hunts other animals.

Roars like a gun being fired,
Moves like a soundless cat,
Is very still like a dead mouse.

Long like a plank of wood,
Huge like a baby elephant,
Paws like a friendly dog.

He is very quiet,
He is quick to get his food,
He is sly to get food.

Can hear his food without moving,
He goes to catch it,
Brings back to secluded spot.

Hunts wild pigs,
And antelope,
And smaller animals.

Jackie Cooke (12)
George Farmer Technology College

ORANGE

Orange is a burning sun,
As hot as a sparking fire.

Orange is a strong tiger,
Looking for its prey.

Orange is a strike of lightning,
Hitting down to the ground.

Orange is my favourite colour.

Orange is a warm deserted beach,
Burning my feet like a cooker.

Orange is an ice-cold drink,
Ahhh . . . it freezes you.

Orange is a butterfly,
Flying to the flower.

Orange is my favourite colour.

Jose Johnson (11)
George Farmer Technology College

ME AND MY MUM

My mum and me get on well,
We cook together,
We wash up and dry together,
Some people say,
'I wish I had your mum'
But I don't say that,
Because me and my mum
Love each other.

Chloe Thurston (11)
George Farmer Technology College

MY BROTHER

My little brother is a pest
He's not one of the best
He's like his mother
A little menace.

He goes out all day and gets all mucky,
Mum's so angry.
Then he comes in for tea and gets mucky all again.
By this time Mum's super angry.

When my aunties come they say what a cute little boy.
If only . . .
If only
They knew the rest.

Rebecca Youngs (11)
George Farmer Technology College

MY PET GERBILS

My mum hates my gerbils,
She says they smell,
'Clean them out!' She says.

They make lots of holes,
They flick the sawdust onto the floor.
That also makes mum angry.

Gerbils eat anything,
Carrots, lettuce and cucumber,
Anything you give them.

I love my gerbils,
Lots and lots,
And lots.

Emma Berry (11)
George Farmer Technology College

I'M AN ELEPHANT

I've got a long, long trunk,
To pick up my food.
I use it to call my calf too.

I love to eat grass, leaves,
And peanuts too.
But that's only when I live in the zoo.

I've got big, wide feet,
To help me on my way.
To the river where I can play.

Huge floppy ears are
Useful to me.
I can hear danger that I can't see.

Melany Clark (11)
George Farmer Technology College

LOST

I'm lost!
I'm in a temporary home.
I hear hurtful cries of youngsters
Calling for their mums and dads,
Why am I here I think all the time?
Why me?
I'm so confused,
I hear constant voices in my head.
I wonder . . .
Will they ever go away
And play around with someone else's feelings?
Does anyone care,
Or am I going to be left here in despair . . . forever?

Jade Harris (14)
George Farmer Technology College

WINTER

It's autumn now
but winter soon.
There'll be crisp white snowflakes
like a big moon.

I love winter, it's really great.
The snow, the sleighs,
it's all too late the snow is here.
I wish it would come all year long.

All the presents on Christmas Day
I love it, I love it, I wish it could stay.
Santa and Rudolf love all our food
Christmas has gone until another year
so goodbye Santa and your deer.

Natalie Hammond (12)
George Farmer Technology College

I'M INVISIBLE

As I sit in my doorway
Freezing and starving,
I try begging but I don't get much,
I sit with a friend,
My only friend,
At night we huddle together to keep warm,
I try not to think about how cold I am,
I wake up in the night,
Only to find a cop shining a light in my doorway,
I then sell the Big Issue but I only get thirty pence,
It isn't enough to keep me going all day,
Everybody then walks by and it's just like I'm invisible.

Jason Dack (12)
George Farmer Technology College

WHY DAD?

Why do you have such a big belly?
Why do you always sit and watch telly?
Why don't you ever drink beer?
Why do you always have fear?
Everyone says you're a chicken, Dad.
Everyone says you're really mad.

Why do you stink of smoke?
Why are you mad about Hollyoaks?
Why are you so thick all the time?
Why are you stealing my toys?
You can't have them, they're mine!
Everyone thinks you're stupid, Dad.
Everyone thinks you're really bad.

Why don't people like you?
They say they hate you and they always go *boo!*
Although they hate you, I love you, Dad.
In my mind you're always the champion.

Rebecca Law (11)
George Farmer Technology College

SHADOWS

Shadows everywhere
Creeping up on you
Trying to watch your every move
Hoping to catch you out
So one day they will
Get you and keep you
Forever in their grasp.

Amy Cooke (12)
George Farmer Technology College

THE BIG ISSUE MAN

He's there again,
Standing with the Big Issue,
Begging he was,
Begging for a quid, just a few pieces of paper,
My mum as always, pays him.
He looks pitiful with his little dog,
Both looking hungry and cold,
He has ragged clothes encrusted with dirt,
Cold, alone without a care in the world
For who he is, what he is to anyone.
Ragged nails, scruffy, long scrawny hair,
I look him up and down looking pitiful for him,
I feel sorry for him,
Give him a few coppers and smile,
He smiles back with his yellow teeth,
I think to myself,
'What a sad life.'

Kerry Lashmar (12)
George Farmer Technology College

HOMELESSNESS

I sit watching people go by,
Their hair nice and dry,
I sit with my dog every day,
My only friend is my dog,
My clothes are holey but nobody cares.
Everybody walks by me like I'm not there,
I'm all scruffy, all I want is a home,
Maybe I'll get a friend one day,
Maybe just maybe!

Samantha Horspool (12)
George Farmer Technology College

ALTON TOWERS

Knock! Knock! Knock!
'What, it's six o'clock!'
'Up you get,' I hear Annie say,
'Come on, ahead of us is a fun-filled day.'

Sleepy eyed with a yawn, yawn, yawn,
Off we go into the dawn,
'Where are we going?' I asked my dad,
'It's a surprise,' he said, 'So you won't be sad.'

The signpost stared up at me,
Alton Towers, whooppee! Alton Towers,
Rides galore, round and round,
High into the air, fast into the ground.

Nemesis, just dangling there,
Twisting, turning, whizzing through the air,
Stomach churning, hair's a mess,
Oblivion - down the hole was simply the best.

Into the dark we raced fast,
In a small car, just fairy lights we passed,
Screams of fear, screams of delight,
Screams for more into the night.

All in all we had a brill day,
Twisting and turning being thrown all ways,
I didn't want to leave Alton Towers,
I could have stayed for hours and hours.

Carly Slator (13)
George Farmer Technology College

THE HOMELESS MAN

He sits there week after week, day after day in the same place.
His manky clothes, rotten teeth and trainers half ripped open.
How do they live life, just begging for money.
I see him every time I go to town.
Not one though, I see more, lots more.
But this one is always sitting there,
Staring into the world, watching the day go by.
No one to love and care for, not a friend to talk to,
All on his own, just him.
I walk by every day, drop 20p in his box,
Not a lot but he always says thanks.
Most people walk on the other side of the road
Still smelling his urine.

Aaron Shepherd (12)
George Farmer Technology College

WHAT IS IT LIKE?

Your hair is as greasy as a chip pan
It's thick, matted and knotted as a ball of string
You don't know when you're next meal is going to come
It could be days or weeks
Your shoes are falling to pieces
What will you do when they are gone
Your skin is dry and cracked
When will you be able to have a wash?
Will you get a bed or somewhere warm to stay for the night?
Your breath smells, your ears are waxy and you look revolting
You ask for money, some give you some,
But mostly they ignore you
Whatever will you do.

Sam Fowler (13)
George Farmer Technology College

MY HOMEWORK

I could not think of a poem
So I guess I'll be going . . .
But . . . I did try so many, many times.
And I did not commit any crimes
But luckily today, I am glad to say . . .
I will bring you my homework another day.
And if that isn't good enough
I'll just have to sleep rough.
Then when it gets into my head
I will write it when I'm in bed.
Then I'll bring it straight to you,
Even if I'm 42!
I will get this homework done.
So here it is, don't worry, I will not run
Because when you read it, you're sure to have fun!

Danny Bell (12)
George Farmer Technology College

THE LADY AND HER DOG

She's walking up and down
trying to keep warm.
She's got long matted hair,
her clothes smell of her dog.
The dog is thin,
people give her money to feed the dog.
Some people gives her a bed and
food for the dog and her.
Her face and hands are dirty
and as people go past she says,
'Spare some change please.'

Heidi Ward (12)
George Farmer Technology College

HOMELESS PERSON

I see him in Peterborough when I go shopping.
He sits with his friend playing his recorder.
Sometimes I wonder where he sleeps at night,
If he sleeps at night.
I wonder what it is like, sitting in a shop doorway
Begging, with no future.
Every day trying to get enough money to eat,
Looking for somewhere to sleep
His music notes are all ripped and dirty,
He puts them in a busted folder.
Walking off somewhere else to beg for money.

Christopher Birchall (12)
George Farmer Technology College

THE NORFOLK BROADS

The wind is rustling in the reeds,
Marsh Harriers soaring on the breeze.
Wherrys slicing through the water.
And no sign of Dad's awful daughter.
Swallows darting, catching flies.
No one knows ahead what lies.
Coots 'kecking,' reed warbler's melodies.
The sound of bird song fills the air.
The halyard clangs upon the mast,
Boat filled water seems utterly vast.
And after all I want to declare -
After reading this poem you'll want to be *there!*

Robin Wilson (11)
George Farmer Technology College

DYING MY HAIR

Every time I dye my hair,
I always get it everywhere,
Purple, red, yellow, green,
Turning orange like a baked bean.

When it goes wrong,
It always goes green,
That's when it looks like a runner bean.

My mum's face goes red,
When she looks at my hair,
Funny looks I always get,
Because I always miss a spot on my head,
Which I always forget!

Helen Mackinder (13)
George Farmer Technology College

WAR

Deep in the bowels of the earth
The roar of the guns could be felt
Men in uniform, smart, dressed to kill
They waited for the order to move and melt
Into the enemies lines all felt ill
And the fear was unspoken in their minds
But old soldiers recognised the signs
Quick smoking of fags, the false smile
The clicking of fingers they all could run a mile
Suddenly the sound stopped
The roar was no more
The radio chattered to life
'Stand down lads it's going to unit 4.'

Rahman Fuad
George Farmer Technology College

THE LONER

Police move me on
from corner to corner;
I have no home,
no known address or phone number.

People move away from me
in case they catch my sadness.
I beg for food, it makes me feel
I have some sort of madness.

My clothes are cast-offs
from the Sally Army;
they don't fit me, just keep me warm,
it helps me not to go barmy.

William Alcock (12)
George Farmer Technology College

THE PELICANARY

I've got a pelicanary,
That sings like that bloke Pavarotti.
Its voice is so good it is scary,
Though it cheats which is terribly naughty.

It has a huge mouth like a dustbin,
Designed to store grub it gets.
But look what it has thrust in,
A machine playing musical cassettes!

Paul Thomas (12)
George Farmer Technology College

HOMELESS POEM

H orrible smelly hair they have
O ne or two people give money as they walk by
M orning and night they sit there
E xpect they feel lonely
L ong knotted muddy hair
E very day they sit there begging
S itting there huddled up in their sleeping bag
S mell catches you as you walk by.

Some people feel sorry
But most people don't.

Emily Ward (12)
George Farmer Technology College

SECRET

Tell me your secret,
I promise not to tell,
I'll guard it safely at the bottom of a well.

Tell me your secret,
Tell me, tell me please.
I won't breathe a word, not even to the bees.

Tell me your secret,
It will be a pebble in my mouth.
Not even the sea can make me spit it out.

Selina Hall (12)
George Farmer Technology College

FEELINGS OF LOSS

Run fast.
Into a slow jog,
My tear is slipping,
Down, down.

Match struck,
Flame is burning,
My anger is boiling,
Growing, growing.

Wind blows,
Thunder crashing,
She's gone away now,
Left, vanished.

Catherine Griggs (13)
George Farmer Technology College

TEENAGER

It's great to be a teenager
A cool and wicked raver
Lots of lovely mood swings
And irrational behaviour.

The anguished cry of poverty
Is always on your lips
Cadging off your folks to buy
Computer games and chips!

Errol Dunham (12)
George Farmer Technology College

Why?

Why is grass so green?
Why is Mum so keen?
Why are trees so tall?
Why is James so small?

Why is it dark at night?
Why is the colour orange so bright?
Why does Timmy live so far?
Why did you want to drive a car?

Why is our surname Clark?
Why do dogs bark?
Why is your favourite colour red?
Why does Mum go to bed?

Why does the sun shine?
Why do people walk in a straight line?
Why is Joe a boy?
Why does Tom have a toy?

Why does poetry have to rhyme
At the end of every line?

Rachael Palmer (11)
George Farmer Technology College

Things To Me

Things to me
Are important;
Like my cat Macavity.
I love it so.
He is as black as coal.
If he wants something
He'll purr at your feet.

Things to me
Are important;
Like my dogs Patch and Grumpy
I love them so.
I spend hour after hour
Playing in the garden with them.

Rachel Walsh (11)
George Farmer Technology College

MY BROTHER

He's only a human
He's only a boy
He's big and strong
And likes to annoy.

Some people think he's bad
Some people say he's mad
But isn't there a bit of fun
Deep inside everyone?

As he hears the gun he begins
To rise, running towards the finishing line.

Winning medals
Scoring goals
Here comes the future
Cole and Scholes

He's an athlete
He's a footballer
But best of all
He's my brother.

Kim Beeken (14)
George Farmer Technology College

TRIBUTE TO STANLEY MATTHEWS

Stanley Matthews was his name
Destroying defences was his game
Scored goals for fun in the rain
Gave a new meaning to the English game.

Played for Blackpool in his prime
Became a Knight in '65
Watching him play others had to swallow their pride
All left backs could do was hide.

First ever world player of the year
All defences could do was fear
He was a man the world loved dearly
But the defenders never got anywhere near him.

Played for thirty-three years
People will never forget his name
First true hero of the English game
He wasn't the only one that suffered his death's pain.

Carl Newell (13)
George Farmer Technology College

UNDER THE STAIRS

I hide each day under the stairs,
Hiding from the big bangs,
Not knowing where my friends are,
Not knowing where my parents are,
I cuddle my ragged brown teddy,
No food, no drink,
No place to go,
When will it end?
But when will I see my parents again?

Leanne Kennedy (13)
George Farmer Technology College

HIGH-TOP HILL

The biting breeze urges me one step closer
to the high-top hill.
Faintly, I can see an image of a tree.
Oak?
It looks like heartless black.
Through the tears it's pulling me forward.

I remember.
Recalling the spiky, green with life. That now looks peaky.
I remember, long ago, when I was a girl.
Long ago, when the hill,
The hill called hope, drew me near.
Calling,
Calling.
Problems drift away absorbed into the neat-cut territory.
I remember, long ago when I was a girl.

A cry of thunder made me fall.
Hands, tremble covered in opaque, inevitable dirt.
The rain made the grand slide, slip, impossible to grip.
Like so many other things - the rain.
It clouds the heavens, leaving only hell and strain.

The moon peaks its weary head,
One last time. Clearing.

I feel the rain trickle like teardrops tampering with my peaky cheek.

I can see it now, the high-top hill. Metamorphasised.

Claire Jackson (17)
Lincoln Christ's Hospital School

WHAT WAS ONCE

I slept with you every night
Even when you weren't there
You'd pollute the oceans of my mind
As I'd surf the waves in despair.

Your grass love threatened
In the summer of mine,
I was suffering disillusion
As you drank me like wine.

Your daisy love I plucked
By my early innocence,
Foreseeing a false fantasy
Crying in your presence.

But your heart was my quicksand,
Your lies were the earth,
It's too late for daisies,
I'm choking on dirt.

Now my heart is your fuel,
You've caused floods of pain,
Now the wind has changed
It's your turn to rain.

Holly Nam (17)
Lincoln Christ's Hospital School

SPELL TO MAKE TEACHERS NICE

A bucketful of kind words
to give to children.

Add a pot of sugar to make them sweet,
a pinch of spice and everything's nice.

A kilogram of patience to deal
with noisy children.

Wrap in a blanket of kindness
to share with everybody.

Calum English (12)
Lincoln Christ's Hospital School

CONSEQUENCE OF A HABIT

The cold holds me back from my goal
to reach the top of my steep hill.

Small caterpillars,
munch at dishevelled plants,
soon they will be butterflies -
able to fly free,
that is what I used to be.

Black skies shadow me over head,
around me lay nature's animals -
weak and feeble,
they could almost be dead.

Hard rains pounds my body
like its hammering me to the ground.
Running over me quickly
coming down fast and thickly.

As I reach the peak of my struggle,
clear mists of breath leave my mouth,
and then evaporate like my habit.

Georgina Pearson (17)
Lincoln Christ's Hospital School

THE SILENT LANDSCAPE...

A desolate place was once full of life,
Fond memories of childhood delight.
Trees still standing but the leaves are not.
The sky is dark with a cloak of clouds.
The grass is swaying from fear of a storm.

I look across the vast open space,
And see a distant paranormal figure,
Of an infant that was as important to me,
As is the sun to our life.

But now the sun has disappeared,
Behind the everlasting horizon,
As if a chapter from a really good book,
Has ended with disillusionment.

The blackness shows no warmth,
Even the stars shine alone in the night's sky,
Bringing no comfort to the eternal sadness,
Of those left behind.

Clair Beaton (18)
Lincoln Christ's Hospital School

ODE TO THE SCHOOL PHOTOS

You are screwed tightly to the cream walls,
All lined up in rows, just like recruits,
The golden sparkling frame surrounding
All the smiling faces.
Everyone's hair is perfection,
The sea of pure white shirts,
Glow with the sun's reflections.

Lisa Dodsworth (15)
Lincoln Christ's Hospital School

MY SONNET

And I laughed when I was younger and all the boys teased,
And when I returned the comment they weren't very pleased,
And I helped my mum on Christmas Day,
And other than that never cleared plates away.

And when I went to school I worked hard,
And when someone criticised I put up my guard,
And when someone had a problem I helped it go away,
And get angry if I couldn't have my say.

And I made my cousin laugh by shouting *boo!*
And I sometimes get mad at everything I do,
And I make my bed every day,
And one time in art I threw some mâché.

Sometimes I am happy and sometimes I am sad,
Sometimes I do good and sometimes I do bad.

Stacey Calvert (15)
Lincoln Christ's Hospital School

RAY

Flat
and thin
creeping carefully
through the water, lethal
as poison, dangerous and daring.
Shark like it descends, moving
freely as the wind, waiting
to pounce, moving
swiftly, while
scaring
prey.

Victoria Hill (11)
Lincoln Christ's Hospital School

ODE TO THE BANANA

I sit, I wait, I want, I need.
I know it is time,
As now I can see forever.
I cannot bear the waiting, I crack and scream
And grunt and shake.

It arrives, a plate of sun.
No time to waste,
It could be lost.

I dive, face first.
Too much joy to chew.
I simply take it all in,
Hands to mouth, hands to mouth.
Coating my face in gold.
Smothering all around, the soft yellow flesh.
I have turned my world into its colour.

I am so happy.
Too happy for silence.
So, again I scream, this time with laughter.
The food is everything, and for that time, it is my life.
These feelings must be shown.

Then up, flying high.
Face is wet, laid down.
Soft,
Sleep,
Dream.

Edward Datta (16)
Lincoln Christ's Hospital School

GROWTH

The sun beats down on the field
As the buds of another new breed come to bloom.
Filled with all the colours of the rainbow
Flowers struggle to find their way.
Too much new growth in one place
Stifling and choking,
The petals soon fall and those who remain
Feed on their rotting bodies.
The weather changes and the colours too.
Growth comes with the sea of rain
And death by drowning in the flood, is not uncommon.
Turbulent changes have diminished the crop,
Those who remain flourish.
A heavy wind sweeps the pretty field.
Bringing the sounds and smells of the city.
The stems tremble in its wake
And the weak are finally broken.
A new breed will be bred to withstand such things,
Whilst a new threat is bred to stop the growth.
As the last flower breathes its last breath,
From this smog-like air, a new shoot appears.

The stifling,
The choking,
The drowning,
The crushing,
The growth.

Matthew Williams (17)
Lincoln Christ's Hospital School

ORCHARD

The air alive and charged
With the hopes and aspirations
Of the dreamers of dreams.

Full of youth and fertility
Fed from the breast
Of a life giving stream.

Smooth bark shoots up
Piercing the grass carpet floor
Still damp from the morning dew.

Stretched out fingers
Lightly pinch the stems of fruits
Ripe and new.

Warm breezes catch the whispers of saints
Whose caresses encourage the green plumes
To quiver in anticipation.

Each breath purifies the soul
As each idea, fantasy, dream, emotion and pleasure
Concentrate into a glowing ball
Burning with the power of sensation.

The sky overhead painted a blue
From the pallet of a king.

At night lit by a million candles
And our glow from within.

A place we've all been
The road we all know
The sights we've all seen
A place we rarely go.

Adam Johnson (17)
Lincoln Christ's Hospital School

WATER AM I?

I roar, yet can be silent.
I'm calm, yet can be violent.
Water am I?

I reign, yet was never crowned.
I'm deep, yet have never drowned.
Water am I?

I am damned, yet am blessed.
I am treasured, yet have no chest.
Water am I?

I creak, yet can be calm.
I wave, yet have no arms.
Water am I?

I gush, yet never cry.
I drip, yet never dry.
Water am I?

I fall, yet also rise.
I see, yet have no eyes.
Water am I?

I smell, yet have no nose.
I ooze, yet also flow.
Water am I?

I'm essential, yet taken for granted.
I'm wasted, yet always wanted.
Water am I?

Water am I?
Water you think?
Water am I.

Patrick Duce (16)
Lincoln Christ's Hospital School

YOUR FACE

Your face gives hope like a
sunrise out of darkness,
The reason to move from my pit.
Fire burns in your eyes and into me
like the unrelenting sun.
Your scent familiar as fresh cut grass
and kiss like honeyed dew.

The day without you
a bleak, barren wasteland,
The sun, taunting me with its brilliance,
withering all in its path,
The charred bodies,
once so full of life,
lie motionless in its wake.

Your return like the moon
beats back the suffocating heat,
With a waterfall of shine over your face
cast by sparkling eyes,
A stream of emotion
flowing over me.

Joanne Kingswood (17)
Lincoln Christ's Hospital School

CAPTURED BY THE VIEW

I swallowed every apple
from the orchard of your soul
each and every one filling an emotional hole.

I didn't know I was trapped
so I didn't try to escape
I was captured by the view
of seemingly beautiful landscape.

You promised me roses yet, somehow,
all I got were the thorns
But now I don't care
because life's too short to mourn.

Annabel Brewer (18)
Lincoln Christ's Hospital School

HAVE A NICE DAY
(THE FORBIDDEN VOICE OF CUSTOMER CARE)

Forty minutes it took me
Forty minutes of painstaking care
     with fifteen minutes to spare
Before the close.

Forty minutes before your time.

     And then from behind the
hats and gloves I watched
     as you charged up to my shiny display
Disregarding my folding, colour -
     Co-ordination and stacking
          with a flick of your wrist.

I ground my teeth as you failed
to find your size in beige
and moved onto cream.

I grimaced nicely
     when you asked me whether you
could try on the cream
     in a size too small

     - by forty minutes.

Tara Wheeler (16)
Lincoln Christ's Hospital School

The Feeling Of Happiness

I walk uneasily through the city
Knowing it is the place where so many have lost their lives
Not to death, that would be less painful
But to another person, be it love or argument
I carry on, blocking out the shouts and tears
Which are so vivid in my mind
The streets are empty but I'm not alone,
I never am.
I'm walking hand in hand with my memories
some, which skip along joyfully, others that bow their heads in sadness.
I'm in a happier place now
My senses sit up and pay attention
The feel of the cold sea on my toes
The smell of fresh air, which surrounds me
The sun will be up soon
I bring my knees up to my chin
And wait for morning to break
Knowing a new day is a new life, somewhere
I've had my day, my first morning,
But the feeling is indescribable if you think the sun rises for you only.
I'm in the forest now.
I lie on the soft moss and look up at the leafy ceiling above me
Their open arms welcome me
When I'm with this other life my sadness drifts into the background,
I can concentrate on what is important
The wind whispers to me
The thunder shouts for me
The lightning lights up my darkest nights.
I can't be lonely when nature is with me
I'm no longer uneasy
I'm home.

Claire Langford (17)
Lincoln Christ's Hospital School

SOMETHING BEYOND WHICH HE CAN SEE

There's a tree on a hill, on its own in the undergrowth
It's a tree but no one knows it yet
A half-eaten apple core, suffocated with featherless pebbles
The naked, racist wind blows through its seed, the same racist wind that
blew the house over into the tide, where a girl once drowned.
The same girl who threw away her suffocated apple core.
And it's only the dark that covers her,
Because the land doesn't want to move.
The waves lap at her feet but she's too cold to touch and the land still
won't come to her rescue, however strong the wind blows.
She's afraid of competition, even the trees are afraid.
He's afraid that there's something beyond which he can see,
and it's coming.
He can smell it in the breeze, not racist, just undecided.
But he can't grow fast enough,
And the pebbles won't protect him any longer because the lands started
moving, wanting to escape the dark that covers everything
But the girl lays cold with a smile on her face
Even though she's dead, she can just see the sky that blinds her.

Kevin Trigg (17)
Lincoln Christ's Hospital School

THE DUCK

It glides through the water with golden webbed feet
Striking fear into the hearts of any creature it should meet,
Sounding its death call, that chilling, wild beat.

A lonely tyrant, it reigns over its land
Millions of minions at its command
An innocent insect walks along a beach band
When crunch, all that remains is sand.

Tom Jeyes (15)
Lincoln Christ's Hospital School

SHARE THE ADVENTURE

Traveller, take me with you,
For neither you nor I belong,
Let us walk together,
To the beat of a muted song.

Child who falls over,
Let me pick you up,
for you cry tears like mine,
Laughter like a bell's chime.

Lonely man are you waiting?
Or may I sit by your side?
Let's travel our minds in silence,
Under the sky's' watchful eyes.

Loser at the side of the cobbled
                              street,
The one with the drunken feet,
Let's weep as freely as the
                              clouds,
Since we have lost what we
                       found,

Just take me with you,
Traveller, let me see you,
Come find me today,
Come ask me and say,

'Will you follow me?
Won't you come too?'
And I'll look up and smile,
'I've been waiting for you.'

So traveller let us stroll,
To the ethnic drum's song,
For I am as blind as a mole,
Let's go to where we belong.

Vahini Sangarapillai (16)
Lincoln Christ's Hospital School

MY ODE TO THE CHAINSAW

The electric version tries its best,
But the petrol saw is better than the rest.

Stihl is the make to buy,
But Black and Decker then ask, why?

Logger saws they have the power,
They cut down trees in half an hour.

Then you get the ten inch too,
That's the home saw for me and you.

The petrol saws they scream and whine,
Whilst the electric ones are quite refined.

The engines are good and strong,
They will run for exceedingly long.

That's my ode to the good old saw,
Rev it, rev it, and rev it some more.

Gregory Boyfield (12)
Lincoln Christ's Hospital School

THE HEADMASTER

Why do we have to knock on the door?
Is it so the Headmaster's aware that we're there?
So he can put away his alien face,
He can't be human, if he was he wouldn't give us a hard time.
Any human being would just laugh at us,
But no, not him, he has to act hard to keep his reputation,
Of the mean old man he really is.
His room's equipped with soundproof walls so no one
Knows when he's having a ball to celebrate the 52nd
Detention handed out today.
Standing on the cloisters acting like he's in charge, when
He knows for a fact he's not,
'Cause if anyone rules the school it's *me!*

Kirsty Blakey (11)
Lincoln Christ's Hospital School

A DIFFERENT WORLD

Out through the door into a different world,
How my feelings transform.
As the breeze brushes past my empty body.
The sharp, cold wind brings a tear to my eye,
Lots of draughty levels that I'm asked to walk.
The green, blooming plants show my healthier side,
Large walls threaten and dominate us.
Long, luscious grass sways like uncut hair,
Deceased small apples lay on the ground,
        Fallen from a height.
Long pale paths that show us the way,
But which route will I take?

Gregory Powis (17)
Lincoln Christ's Hospital School

THE LIBRARIAN

What does Miss do
When no one's around?
Does she write new books
That no one's found?
Will anyone know
What she does every day?
Does she sit and read books
Or chuck them away?
Does she climb up the shelves
Or shout out loud?
Does she write out fines
Of which she's proud?
Can you answer my questions?
Can the answer be found?
Oh what does Miss do
When no one's around?

Rosie Cole (11)
Lincoln Christ's Hospital School

THE GLOW WORM

He softly slips along the ground,
His graceful glide the only sound,
His steady stamina knows no bounds.

The dull, grey soil crumbles below,
As his smooth, sleek body, in a rhythmic flow,
Emits a faint and mystical glow.

Emma Seward (15)
Lincoln Christ's Hospital School

My Scary Poem

I was walking through the graveyard,
With the wind whistling through my hair,
I was certainly expecting something to give me a
great big scare.

Then I heard a creepy noise,
The snapping of a branch.
So I went over to see what was there,
And if it would raise a hair.

What I found was a ewe tree,
It certainly looked like a mystery.
So in a rage of horror, I began to climb it,
Up and up I went to see what I could see.

When I got to the top
I heard a rattling chain,
In my fright I lost my grip and I was never seen
Again.

Alasdair Robinson (12)
Lincoln Christ's Hospital School

My Dog

Piercing eyes like a needle.
Legs are short as a hand.
Tail moves like washing on a windy day.
His neck is like an arm.
His eyes are like sunflowers, dancing around all day long.
His body is thick like a tree trunk.
Fur is as white as a polar bear
And his nose is like a wet wipe.

Carly Haddock (12)
St Hugh's CE School

CAT

Eyes like glitter
Ears like flowers
Nose is like velvet
Tail is like a bush
Claws are like little thorns
Fur is like cotton wool.

Stacey Goodge (12)
St Hugh's CE School

LADY

You are a lady sweet and kind
was never face so pleased in my mind
I did but see you passing by
and yet I love you till I die
give us a smile before we part
and I'll keep it in my heart.

Terri-Anne Foster (12)
St Hugh's CE School

DAY AND NIGHT

The crescent pale moon
candle light, yellow stars,
dancing in the sky.

The sunshine, shines bright
like a bright candle light,
glowing through the day.

Tammy Eldred (12)
St Hugh's CE School

HAUNTED HOUSE

Haunted house on a haunted hill.
Five visitors came to stay
Two people lived there
No one knew what was under the house
Not even them
The five visitors decided to explore
Up, up, went the trap door.
The smell was damp, it was dark and cold.
Don't go the owners called.
Too late.

Haunted house on a haunted hill.
Five visitors went to stay and never came back.

Mark Ward (11)
St Hugh's CE School

THE SEA AT NIGHT

The storm broke out in the middle of the night,
And the terrible wind attacked the sea.
The sea crashed against the powerful rocks,
Back and forth, back and forth.
Shining and glistening in the moonlight.
Ripples of foam gushing from its mouth,
As it swallows the menacing rocks.
The dark of night shadows its form,
The light of the moon shows piercing eyes of the
Monster hidden within.
The great storm died away leaving the sea calm
And dead as the darkness surrounding it.

Jennifer Cain (11)
Skegness Grammar School

THE CAULDRON

Wallowing around the circumference,
The defences in quagmire,
The sparse foliage of stark trees
and black weapons litter the crucible rim,
Cold water slumps in every featureless depression
and shivers at the gun bursts.

Each side watching the other,
The black eyes of the machine guns staring hungrily into the bowl,
Each muzzle ravenously drooling wisps of smoke,
A rat flounders in a boot print,
Clambering out onto a dead soldier's rifle,
Knocking the safety catch,
Click,
A thunderous roar churning and kneading,
Mud on mud hurling and heaping,
The bank riddled with black and yellow,
Whines and whistles as every nervous soldier,
Looses off at the illusive attackers,
The firing fades and the trees grow foliage,
Thick clusters of black and grey leaves,
Rising slowly off their skeletal trunks.

And now the trees have foliage,
Lush and green,
And in the handsome field next to the village,
There is a slight depression,
And still old men out on a stroll,
Will skirt slowly and widely round,
And then move off quietly into the woods,
Pulling a tissue from their pockets.

Tom Barton (17)
Skegness Grammar School

A NEW LIFE IN THE MILLENNIUM

A new life in the millennium,
The world's gone totally strange,
Everything has its own imagination
Some good things still remain.

On the last night of the millennium,
Century, decade, too,
There I were sat wondering what I was going to do
My computer would crash I'd turn out in a rash,
What was I going to do?

A new life in the millennium,
Whatever would happen next?
Everyone had gone mad, nothing to help them
Whatever would happen next?

The time had passed, it was the middle of the year,
Things were beginning to get back to themselves,
Until they invented all sorts of things,
Such as little elves.

A new life in the millennium
The first year had finally passed,
Coming to the year 2001 now,
My birthday . . . at last.

Charlotte Bradbury (13)
Skegness Grammar School

MY BEDROOM

My bedroom is a state,
I'm peeling off the wallpaper I hate.
There's bits of paper flying around,
Until they settle down to the ground.

My bedroom is a hit,
Where my friends can come and sit.
My bedroom used to be empty,
Ready to paint a plenty.

Samantha Oakley (11)
Skegness Grammar School

MY BEST FRIEND

My best friend is extremely caring,
And I'm sure that she's obsessed with sharing.
We never really, ever fell out,
And I don't really like to, 'cause boy can she shout.

She never lets me put myself down,
I have to tell her the cause of my long frown.
My best friend is such a big star,
In the future, I'm sure she'll go far.

She is always there,
To care and to share.
To hug when I'm sad,
And a comfort when I'm bad.

My best friend is very kind,
And if you break her toys, she won't even mind!
She always has a smile on her face,
Even when she trips on her own shoelace!

I hope that we will stay friends forever,
Because my life is more fun when we're together.
We stick together through thick and thin,
Through prep and detention, lose or win.

Lizzie Schofield (11)
Skegness Grammar School

DREAMING OF A GREEN HALLOWE'EN

As witches cackle around the cauldron chanting,
 Twist the bones and then the back,
  Give him fire as black.

When a bat,
Just like that,
 Came flying down and turned into a vampire,
  With a loud screech.

When a devil,
With the revel,
 Fired himself up with raging red horns and said,
  'Excuse me, any chance of a cup of tea?'
When a ghost with a pumpkin,
Flying like a dumpling,
 Came down to the ground with a ghostly
  Haunt,
   Oi, have you seen devil and revel,
With a crash,
Then a flash,
 They all mysteriously disappeared.

Rebecca Johnson (11)
Skegness Grammar School

CATS

Cats have bright, shiny eyes,
They also have nine lives,
Cats come out to prey at night,
With their eyes burning bright.

Cats come out to pounce and play,
After playing with stuffed mice all day,
Trying to catch an unwary mouse,
Who decided to pop out of his little house.

The cat moves slow trying not to be seen,
With his eyes shimmering among the green,
To make a sudden movement would scare the mouse,
Scurrying back into his cosy house.

Laura Geaghan (12)
Skegness Grammar School

JUST ME AND MY HORSE

The wind was rushing through my hair,
Wherever I want to go she will take me there,
The rabbits, the bees and all of the trees,
Take me there *please, please, please!*

We will ride to the stars,
Pluto, Jupiter or even Mars,
We shall compete in lots of races,
And see the children with smiling faces,
I can see it now.

We shall become worldwide famous,
And get our picture printed in the papers,
Black Beauty her name, shall be,
Just Black Beauty and me.

Then one day it all shall end,
And she shall always be my dearest friend,
She has retired and lives with me,
I often ride her down to the sea.

The many trophies shining bright,
They sparkle in the middle of the night,
That remind me of
   Just me and my horse.

Sophie Bray (11)
Skegness Grammar School

BOND POEM

Bond races in his Aston Martin,
giving his foe a punch on the chin.
His code name is 007,
people wonder if he'll ever go to Heaven.

In 'Goldeneye',
he was shot into the sky.
I think the best thrill,
was in 'A View to a Kill'.

He loves his Martinis
and women wearing bikinis.
His name is . . .
Bond . . . James Bond.

Callum Vine (11)
Skegness Grammar School

I WISH I COULD . . .

I walk around, all day and night,
Watching birds in their flight.
I wish that I could fly myself,
Jump off a very high wooden shelf.
Wonder, wonder, all I can do,
Nearer I go towards a cliff,
And the sea breeze is all I can sniff.
I look around for birds in flight,
Seeing if any come in my sight.
Nearer and nearer, it looks so steep,
Splashing water, looks so deep.
One step at a time I go,
One step . . . two step . . . three step . . . go.

Helen Jones (11)
Skegness Grammar School

MY FAVOURITE POSSESSIONS

Its shiny paint,
Its glowing light,
That is why I like my bike,
It overshadows my sister's trike.

Its amazing brain,
It's a bit of a pain,
But it would not be the same,
Without my computer.

It's furry, it's grey,
It's home every day,
It likes to stay,
Furrying around, it's my rabbit.

David James Hill (11)
Skegness Grammar School

DICK TURPIN

When travelling on a journey,
People lived with their fear,
That one day the famous highwayman
Dick Turpin would appear.
He would pull out his gun,
Take all their jewels and money.
He may only be the innkeeper's son,
But no one thought he was funny.
He was hanged in York,
After murdering a man,
No more Dick Turpin,
So travel all you can!

David Smith (12)
Skegness Grammar School

MY BEST FRIEND

My best friend is always there,
We play together and always share.
She always helps me when I'm stuck,
And in return I give her my tuck.

My best friend is very pretty,
Especially when we go into the city.
We shop all day till we can carry no more,
Breathing a sigh of relief as we go through the door.

My best friend loves her horse,
She even went on a riding course.
We go swimming together on a Tuesday night,
And when she goes under she gives me a fright.

My best friend is simply the best,
She never, ever stops to rest.
As she is cleaning her room which is always messy,
But the best thing about her never gets stressy.

Emily Rose (11)
Skegness Grammar School

I HAVE A DREAM

I have a dream
To be Bond for a day,
All the gadgets and guns, there's no dismay.
Running down corridors, meeting some women,
Then again all this ends with a killing.
I have a dream, to be James Pond,
Oh no, sorry, Bond, James Bond.

Ben Newman (11)
Skegness Grammar School

WITCHES

With bright green, curly hair
Wicked smiles and a horrible stare
In their cauldrons horrid smelly ingredients go
Disgusting rats' tails, dragons' brains and a frog's toe.

Using toads' skin green lipstick
Applying fungi eye shadow
Bright green hair dyes
And gruesome purple liner for their eyes.

Wearing dark black robes
With bright pink holes
Ripped, torn and dirty
Smelly, worn and murky.

I think I've decided to stay away from witches
And their horrible faces all grey
Their disgusting make-up, clothes and pointed hats
Not to mention their smelly pet bats.

Anne-Marie Quincey (12)
Skegness Grammar School

A TRIP

A trip in the V-Dub camper,
the best I've had in years,
down to Fistrel Beach,
the surf spot of the year.
A carpet of surfers over the sea
catching their wave
as if it was meant to be.
A journey that has end, it's sad I have to go.
Goodbye my perfect dream, back to reality.

William Forster (12)
Skegness Grammar School

TIME

Tick-tock, tick-tock time goes by,
Never missing a second even in the darkest sky,
Tick-tock, tick-tock time goes on,
No one can stop it going on.
Tick-tock, tick-tock time goes forward,
On time we can rely.

Ding-dong, goes the hour bell,
It's two o'clock and you can tell,
Ding, dong, goes the second hand,
Slower, than the first round and round.

The clock has twelve numbers which help us tell the time,
You can rely on time even in mime,
Seconds, minutes, hours and days,
Months and years and decades.

Time goes on as you do anything,
Short, big or small,
So think before you waste it.

Leah Gray (12)
Skegness Grammar School

THE THOUGHT

I was standing on a bridge at midnight,
When a thought came into my head,
What a total fool I was for standing there,
When I could have been fast asleep in bed.

I was sitting in the park on Monday,
When that thought came back to me,
How silly I was for sitting there,
When I could have been having my tea.

I was in the living room watching TV,
When my mum came and said to me,
'You know these strange thoughts you're having,
Maybe a doctor you should go and see.'

Viki Bartlett (11)
Skegness Grammar School

MY ROOM

I had a lovely dream last night, of having a tidy room,
But next day when I woke up, I found my dream untrue.

It was still just like a bomb shelter, toy soldiers dead on the floor,
I got out of bed and jumped and screamed,
Then there was a heart stopping knock on the door.

'I wish this hadn't happened,' I said.

The door opened wide with a glass-shattering scream,
'I told you, get ready for school,
This bedroom is still like a year's worth of mess,
And you still haven't cleaned Bernie's drool.'

Bernie makes me embarrassed sometimes,
But I still think he's a really cool dog,
Though my friends usually laugh at him,
Because he wees on the way to school.

For some reason my bedroom is never tidy,
It's usually always a mess,
I always get told off by my mum,
It's worse than a pigsty she mainly says,
So the statement I reply with is . . .

Too rude to hear!

James Housam (12)
Skegness Grammar School

SPELLBOUND CAKE

To make a cake for my friend
I will be in the kitchen until no end
Putting in delicious things
I might even add a little bat wing

Rats' tails
Snakes' scales
A little white dove
I'm sure she'll love

Frogs' legs
Wooden pegs
Slimy snails
And puppy dog tails

An old piece of kipper
With a pinch of pepper
A rotten Quaver
To add more flavour

Witches' hair
But I must take care
As it will boil and bubble
And I will be in great trouble

A little dead mole
Wrapped in a buttered roll
Add a grubby football
From the old town hall

A pinch of salt
And a metal bolt
It's time I brought this cake to a finish
Just after I add a pinch of spinach.

Kerry Rogers (11)
Skegness Grammar School

LOVE

Love, tell me what it is?
He whispered in my ear.
Love is as soft as a raindrop,
As sharp as a spear.

Sometimes it makes you want to laugh
And then it makes you cry.
Sometimes you feel your life is bliss
And then you want to die.

You give someone your love,
When it's been taken from the skies above
And then they feel the need to give it back
Because their love in their hearts lacks.

They give it to you by their eyes,
Flowing through you like the clouds in the skies,
Through your brain, back to your heart,
Where it was at the start.

You know some day there will be another,
Someone you'll love as much as the other.

When the process starts again,
You know your love is on the mend
And you're sure this one
Will never end.

Now you're back,
A new best friend,
A heart to care for,
The love to lend.

Camille Butt (13)
Skegness Grammar School

THE STREET

As I walked down the street,
I saw cute little dogs with fuzzy feet.
I saw ugly babies crying in their prams,
I saw mean children planning their evil plans.

As I walked down the street,
I saw a fire of blazing heat,
I saw drunk teenagers drinking,
I saw fat builders building.

As I walked down the street,
I saw drivers stuck in their seat,
I saw a toy in a shop that was very cool,
I saw an ugly clown that looked a fool.

That's what I saw in the . . .
  Street!

Ben Amis (11)
Skegness Grammar School

THE CHURCHYARD

Twilight,
A chill wind blowing,
Trees bending,
Crispy leaves swirling.
Clouds blowing across the moon.
An owl hooting,
Dilapidated gravestones, all shapes and sizes,
Dying flowers,
Neglected grass.
A lonely old woman staring silently at her husband's grave.
Sadness.

James Glenn (12)
Skegness Grammar School

MADNESS

If you were to perceive madness
Would you see a friend in me
Or perhaps an evil concoction of notion
Would you feel a shivering spine by my gladness
You wouldn't see me, just what you behold me to be.

I'm not your twisted mind type
Nor your foul friend, I am not you
I am but me and I am alone
My thoughts may not be ripe
As I never grew.

Your perception is the one twisted thing here,
That head of yours may turn away,
Yet I see your fear, I feel your distrust
Though I know not why you fear,
For all the things I say
Cannot break the curse of your intrust.

Joseph Hippey (13)
Skegness Grammar School

DRAGON

D   ragon breath we know can stink, it
R   eally is so vile, it stinks of sweaty socks
A   nd rotten vegetables, with its
G   ruesome face
O   n its big fat head, is
N   ot very nice at all.

James Pass (12)
Skegness Grammar School

SEASONS

Spring begins with growing daffodils all bright
                                    yellow in the sun,
Baby lambs are born, then they play in the field and
                                    have lots of fun.

Then the weather becomes warmer which means
                                    summer has just begun,
With ice lollies and playing on the beach but watch out for
                                    the burning sun.

Autumn brings winds to make all the leaves fall,
And with the festival of Hallowe'en, it's a spooky time for all.

When the snow begins to fall, we know it is wintertime,
With Christmas trees and presents galore,
All the excitement comes to a fore.

Linsey Abbott (12)
Skegness Grammar School

AUTUMN DAYS

A is for the autumn leaves, all golden brown and crisp,
U is for the umbrellas being blown inside out,
T is for the trees which sway in the cool autumn breeze,
U is for the uttering voices, carried in the wind,
M is for the misty morning, I wake up to and stare,
N is for the noise of leaves, underfoot.

D is for the darkness, that rapidly descends,
A is for the apples, ripe and ready to be picked,
Y is for the yawns, in front of warm, log fires,
S is for the season of bonfires, ghosts and ghouls!

Scott West (12)
Skegness Grammar School

CHRISTMASTIME

A   is for an appetising Christmas dinner,

M   is for merry men you will see over this festive time,
E   is for enjoyment for all when you receive your presents,
R   is for making your new year's resolution,
R   is for rolling snowballs out of the ground,
Y   is for yawning waiting for Santa to appear,

C   is for Christmastime fun had by all,
H   is for having a hot bath on the cold winter morning,
R   is for rejoicing with your family,
I   is for indulging in the Christmas feast,
S   is for snowman which you have fun to make,
T   is for the Christmas tree shimmering with decorations,
M   is for many festive cheers with your friendly folk,
A   is for the angel whom sits atop the Christmas tree,
S   is for Santa on his sleigh delivering children's presents.

Shane Story (12)
Skegness Grammar School

POEM

The stands are full, the crowd waits for the game to begin
Fans from both teams want their players to win
The teams come out, they start to shout
The game has begun
The ball in the net, a roar from the crowd
But the referee said it was disallowed,
The ball is won,
A tackle is done,
Ninety minutes has gone,
But the best team won.

Robert Taylor (13)
Skegness Grammar School

CHRISTMAS DAY

C is for Christmas tree that is so bright,
H is for happiness, everyone's delight,
R is for red, the colour of the lights,
I is for indigo, the colour of the sky,
S is for songs that carol singers sing,
T is for toys that Santa Clause brings,
M is for magic that all children feel,
A is for the angel so pretty on the tree,
S is for snow that falls and covers me.

D is for decorations that hang from the roof,
A is for amber, the colour of the fire,
Y is for Yule log that burns so bright.

Darius Corry-Smith (12)
Skegness Grammar School

A DOG'S LIFE

I am a dog called Alfie,
I like to run about,
I like to chase my ball,
And catch it in my mouth.

My master thinks it's funny,
When I jump up in the air,
Sometimes I land upon my back.

When I am home and in my bed,
My master calls and strokes me,
Then we have a little cuddle,
And off we go to bed.

Luke Makepeace (11)
Skegness Grammar School

DREAMING

I love to sleep and daze into tireless dreams,
They swirl around inside my head,
Pounding smashing against my brain.
I dream of bursting colours senseless pictures,
Of floating weightlessly in the clouds,
Flying, diving through the mountains and trees,
Up in the sky away from the clouds,
Free to let my spirit take me,
Some dreams are monstrous and evil and wake
Me from my slumber,
Others I wish could last forever,
Most I can never remember,
I love to dream.

Jeremy Harding (12)
Skegness Grammar School

THE DRAGON

I discovered a dragon in a shell
It breathed flames like fiery hell
Its eyes glinted in the sun
Whilst flying round having fun.

It finally came down to the ground
And tripped and fell with a great bound
It quickly got back up again
And set ablaze its brand new den.

It made its home in a cave
Where the sea washed wood up with every wave,
It used the wood for a fire
And hung its washing to get dryer.

Daniel Oakley (13)
Skegness Grammar School

My Dream Adventure With Buffy Summers

I suddenly fell asleep and had entered the world of Buffy,
She's very good looking though, but she's quite a toughie.
As I was trying to fight vampires, armed with my lucky stake,
Buffy comes and helps me, from my fate.
I helped her and she helped me, boy weren't we a team,
I could say that this was one hell of a dream.
As we both went to Sunnydale High School, we went into the library
to see the whole gang,
As I opened the door into the library it started off like a colossal bang.
Met Xander, Willow, Oz and Giles,
I can't believe I met them after a journey of so many miles.
Night had come and Buffy and I went walking,
Armed with knives and crossbows and stakes, who knows what was
watching us stalking.
Then out came Spike and Harmony and many more,
I said to Buffy, 'This will be easy, just like killing a wild boar.'
We killed all the vampires, sending them back to hell.
Then I heard the sound of 'Dream over', coming from the bell.
As I turned to the gate, where it all ends,
I finally said 'I'll see you tomorrow night, goodbye friend.'

Charles Day (13)
Skegness Grammar School

The Sea

The sea is a large expanse,
In it lives mammals and fish and sea creatures,
It covers the majority of the planet,
The sea has lots of different features.

It can be rough, it can be calm,
It can appear inviting,
Always approach the sea warily,
It can be ferocious and frightening.

The tide can rise and the waves crash down,
It can suck and drag you in,
It is strong and fierce for any human being
And it is a battle you will rarely win.

But other times it's peaceful, calm and serene,
The waves lap gently on the shore,
This is when it's safe to venture in,
But beware it may turn once more.

Callum Ferguson (12)
Skegness Grammar School

ANIMAL FARM

I walked through the gates of the muddy farm
And there I saw, to my alarm,
A little lamb wandering all alone,
As cute as he was, I wanted to bring him home.
But then something huge was coming my way,
A horse was galloping near, wanting to play.
As big as it was I was a little scared,
So I stayed away, just watching I glared.
I was looking for the pigs, which interest me the most,
But none I could find, wait! What was that beside the post?
Yes one little pink pig followed by a bunch,
They were so cute, but I was hungry, when's lunch?
When we had finished the picnic so divine,
The sheep were our next animal in line,
Their little bodies covered in fluff,
They look like clouds and all that stuff,
Our day ended when the rain fell through,
I was so wet, I didn't know what to do.
I went home in the car,
That was the best day I have ever had by far.

Laura Hill (13)
Skegness Grammar School

DREAMS

Dreams are forever,
Like water in the sea.

Dreams of stars and plants,
Of oriental chimes.

Japanese women in Kimonos,
Yin yangs in the trees.

All stay forever,
Forever in your dreams.

Magic over waterfalls,
Pogodas and dragons.

Witches over cauldrons,
As planes go round the sun.

Safe under cover of your bed.

Dreams are forever,
Forever in your mind.

Kimberley Gill (12)
Skegness Grammar School

DREAMS . . .

Lyin' in your bed,
The moon shines bright,
Thoughts in your head,
All through the night.

Dreams come and go,
Happy or sad.
Dreams that you know,
Are gonna make you mad!

Dreams can come true,
Sometimes, maybe not.
Some people have a few,
Some people have a lot.

Dreams can be boring,
The worst you've ever had.
You might dream you're snoring,
You might dream you're mad.

Cheryl Bark (13)
Skegness Grammar School

CRAIG DAVID

Craig David is the king
I wish I could sing like him.

I listen to his music every day
The beats of his songs I would like to play.

He's cool and stylish
To be like him, I wish.

He's famous and rich
Won awards for his hits.

My favourite song is Seven Days
I listen to it in many ways.

On my Walkman, CD player and on the TV
The words I remember easily.

I love the songs he plays
Remember this goes out to all the DJs.

Liam Brader (13)
Skegness Grammar School

WEMBLEY

The grass is green,
The lines are white,
The crowds are keen,
The scores are tight,
The towers are tall,
The kits are clean,
They're soon to be small,
The other team's mean,
Too many years of hurt,
Since the Jules Remay was here,
On the seats is dirt
And some remains of beer,
The atmosphere builds up,
A new beginning starts,
A new stadium to be built for the World Cup,
All the time football in our hearts.
The memories of Argentina and Germany,
With all our famous names,
The wins and losses many,
Let's all just hope England wins the rest of its games.

Danny Clarke (13)
Skegness Grammar School

MY FAMILY

I've got a brother called Kyle
Who's got a very big smile,
I've got a sister called Hannah,
Who likes to play the piano.

I've got a dad called Paul,
Who's extremely tall,
I've got a mum called Nicki
Who is always very sicky.

I've got a cousin called Cairo
Who decided to eat a Biro
I've got a step cousin called Jade
Who gambled all her money in the arcade.

I've got an uncle called Jansen
Who's very handsome,
I've got an aunty called Louise,
Who's got a very deadly disease.

Kayleigh Broddle (12)
Skegness Grammar School

THE BEACH

The sun
The sea
The sand
The wind that howls and growls,
Stings the skin
And the blood within.

The birds
The kites
The dogs
The boats moored upon the land
Nets blowing and expanding.

The waves
The pebbles
The crabs
The shoal of fish
Unaware of the storm on land.

Joanna Matthews (12)
Skegness Grammar School

THE 14TH HOLE

Down slides the tee
Piercing sodden turf.
The wayward white ball
Glares up from below.
Which way will it go?

The glistening green target's
Magnetic force
Teases me, lures me,
Urges me try.
Which way will it fly?

One hundred and sixty yards -
A six or maybe five.
The club face taunts the ball
'Prepare for the connection!'
In what direction?

The wind wails
As the billowing flag
Points to the danger
Of selfish sand.
Where will it land?

All I can do is wait . . .
Anticipate . . .
Hope . . .

Damn!

Alex Colman (12)
Skegness Grammar School

UNDERWATER LIFE

Many fish deep in
The ocean,
Each one glimmering
From the sunlight
Above,
Emotions running high,
Life running low,
Many fish deep,
Deep in the ocean.

Many fish deep in
The ocean,
Each one swimming
Through the calm sea,
People don't understand
What's happening under there,
Do they really care?

Many fish deep in
The ocean,
Having a life,
Well maybe so
Some big fish,
Some small fish,
But each one hoping
For the same,
An underwater life.

Sarah-Jayne Smith (12)
Skegness Grammar School

SPACE

5, 4, 3, 2, 1 . . .

The rocket launched
I went through the atmosphere
The rocket's skin glowed like a red fire
I was free,
I was in space
I could see all Earth's beauty,
From America to Australia
Then I landed,
I drifted onto the surface on the moon
I had got there so soon.
Yet I had been up there so long
I felt like Neil Armstrong.

Jason Crooks (13)
Skegness Grammar School

THE MOUSE

Tiny, grey and small,
It creeps across the hall
And into the dining room
It zooms:
Dodging the sleeping cat on the chair
And behind the bookcase there
It slips into its hole,
Tiny, grey and small,
It curls up in a ball . . .
            . . . and sleeps.

The mouse!

Rachel Marriott (13)
Skegness Grammar School

A FISH'S WORLD

A fish will swim in big blue waters,
It has very special features,
When a fisherman drops his hook,
The fish tries to be a crook,
It goes after the worm,
But it gets caught and will squirm,
It may be in a lot of pain,
But it didn't eat its little brain.

Bigger fish will try to eat it,
But it is fast so it can hide quiet,
Its skin is covered in slime
And it takes it a little time
To swim around looking to eat
It can see human's great big feet,
Then it will swim to the other side,
Where pike wait for the tide.

Fish think their life is good,
In the murky waste and mud
When they're chased there is no tears,
Even though their death is near,
Due to this most fish fear,
Is the water dark or clear,
In this place their life begun
And here they die as one.

Under its gigantic fin,
Little fish will enter in,
The worm in water seems to fly
Although to fish it will never die,
And if they had one wish
'No more lands' said the fish.

Jed Stainton (13)
Skegness Grammar School

THE NOU CAMP

Off to Barca we go,
To see them play
Against the kings,
Who are expected to win.

They have travelled across Spain,
To be here now,
They are ready to get changed,
And walk down that famous tunnel.

They are ready to go,
To battle it out,
This famous match,
Won't let us down.

Off we go,
The whistle has been blown,
Goals are flying in
Kluivert, Figo, Cocu.

Half-time.

We get the snacks,
Burgers, crisps, soup,
The whistle goes,
We're off again.

It's exciting again,
Shots and goals are flying,
Carlos, De Boer, Raul,
The whistle blows,
It's the last few seconds of the game.

Penalty!
Kluivert steps up,
Goal!
It's all over,
The greatest win
For ages!

Sean Robert Chamberlain (13)
Skegness Grammar School

THE MATCH

I went to the match
To watch the Arsenal play,
They took on Man Utd,
Oh this will be a great day.

We went really close,
With a Bergkamp shot,
It was a sunny day,
We all felt hot.

I was feeling really good,
Until Man Utd scored,
A Sheringham header,
Made us all feel bored.

But super sub Henry,
Saved the day with his sole,
A curling strike,
Which ended in a goal.

Edward Suich (12)
Skegness Grammar School

DEXTERS

Her name was Jasmine,
She was as black as night itself.
Though I always call her mine,
She walks around at night by stealth.
She's so beautiful, I told him,
I can't resist her large brown eyes.

In the morning I go to see her.
The song of her voice meets my
Ears and wakes me into running there.
That day went well until she licked my ear,
I went running home sobbing, oh so much,
For she had a baby by her side.

That night I dreamt of her,
The black hair that was so, so shiny.
In the morning I went to see her,
Oh her food was so nice.
Her tail swished the flies off her back and then she sang,
Oh the Dexter's song is so great.

The cow and her calf sang so well.

Adrian Lockwood (13)
Skegness Grammar School

THE ELEPHANT

The elephant creature is big and round,
In the jungle they just wander around.
But what does an elephant keep in his ear?
12 currant buns, the answer's so clear!

The elephant creature is worldwide known,
For his skin is every known grey tone.
But what does an elephant keep in its trunk?
A bit of fluff and the rest is junk!

The elephant creature hangs around in groups,
His curly tail is the shape of two loops.
But what does an elephant keep in his toes?
Everything and all that he can't fit in his nose!

The elephant creature never forgets,
For if he did he would start to regret.
But what does an elephant keep in its belly?
A piece of toast and a bowl full of jelly!

Sarah Helmore (13)
Skegness Grammar School

THE BUG IN MY ROOM

Lying in my bed so snug,
Through the darkness I see a bug.
It is huge, it is black, it is hairy, it is fat.
I scream, I shout, I thump, I yell,
Come and save me from this hell!
Dad comes in so bold, so stern,
With words so loud, with words so firm.
He said, go to sleep you silly girl,
And turned around in one fail swirl.
I hear my bedroom door slam,
It goes with an almighty bang.
My dressing gown on the bedroom door,
Falls off in a heap on the bedroom floor.
I know the bug is still near,
I don't think it will disappear.
I look at the bug and it seems to look back
And then it disappears down a crack.
I sigh with relief because now I can go to sleep.
Goodnight . . .

Vanessa Harlow (12)
Skegness Grammar School

THE SOLDIER

Lying bloodstained in a poppy field,
The soldier moaned his final plead,
'Can anybody hear me . . . please?'
But only grunts and groans returned his cry.

Right leg blown off by a grenade,
His ribs deformed or broken,
Eyeball gauged out with the enemies knife,
Bloody face, legs, arms and hair.

All around him lay more soldiers,
Dead or on the way;
With guns held tightly in their hands,
Or knives interposed in their remains.

If that were you
Then surely you would think there is point of war,
If you would you're right,
The only thing war can end with is people's blood
And tears.

Annabel White (13)
Skegness Grammar School

THE BUILDING STRAIGHT AHEAD

Looking out into the dusky twilight,
Standing under a blanket of stars,
Staring ahead at what was before me,
An ancient building with wrought iron bars.

Staring so much it brought me to wonder,
Of tales of mystery and imagination,
From times gone by and up to the present,
Now the house stood in a state of devastation.

Stretching high, up into the heavens,
Towers pointing up into the sky,
Surrounded by a forest of trees,
It gave me a haunting feeling that would never die . . .

Heather Newham (13)
Skegness Grammar School

MY MOTHER

My mother is a special person,
She is always there for me.
When I get home from a day at school
Mum greets me with a cup of tea.

Mum listens to my problems
And tries to sort them out
I don't always like her suggestions
But she carries a lot of clout!

I am often rude and cheeky,
I don't always treat her the way I should.
I don't do what she asks of me,
But one day I promise I'll be good.

I tease my sister all the time
And drive her up the wall.
I love to see her get really wound up
But Mum doesn't like it at all!

When I'm older I'll try to be all that you want,
Be kind, be thoughtful and full of the peace of the dove,
Be generous in the ways I know
And our house, Mum will be full of love!

Jack Kennell (13)
Skegness Grammar School

THROUGH THE EYES OF A CLOUD

Through the eyes of a cloud everything is perfect.
The tremendous waterfall filled with amazing secrets.
Beautiful flying fish shooting with all the colours of the rainbow.

A child in the Olympics with confidence.
The confidence of a soldier about to go into war.
Nervousness, fear and anxiety leave him
and suddenly he dashes faster than a swift gazelle
and a prowling cheetah.

A lion's heart, master of the jungle beats the rhythm of life,
a slithering snake winds round a thick trunk of a tree
like a flexible vine does to a thin branch.

An artist paints all his emotions into his painting.
His painting is made up of thoughts, feelings, emotions.
His painting is the best of all.

The wind howling like a ferocious werewolf in the forest.
The deep, dark forest turns into a playful tune
that a happy piper plays on his flute.
The golden rays lighten up the face of Mother Earth.

When it rains listen carefully to the rhythm.
Perfection, love, kindness.
Perfection, love, kindness and then you will know
through the eyes of a cloud, all it sees is love.

Beth Atiba (11)
Skegness Grammar School

THE PASSIONATE TRAINSPOTTER TO HIS LOVE

Please come and join me, oh yes you,
Bring your rain mac and notebook too,
We'll sit and wait by the railway line
And look for train number twenty-nine.

We'll sit upon the gravelled stone
And talk of the train we shall own,
I'll put the coal into the fire
And you shall do what you desire.

Your bobble hat will look so sweet,
Perched on your head so nice and neat,
The trainspotter's manual we will share,
Each number seen will show I care.

We'll meet daily at the station,
Proving our love to the nation,
Watching as all the trains arrive,
Keeping our love for trains alive.

Blue Biro's lined in my pocket,
As old as Stephenson's Rocket,
I will provide the flask of tea,
Whilst you sit cosy next to me.

My love for trains it has no end
But love for you, you can depend,
Please come and join me, oh yes you,
Bring your rain mac and notebook too.

Emily Skipworth (17)
Skegness Grammar School

MY CAT

My cat, he's small and cute;
Can you imagine him in a suit.
With his little ears and paws,
He'd do a dance for an applause.
He runs around with a mouse,
Normally brings it in the house.
He sleeps on my bed,
On a pillow near my head.
He cries all night,
Until I turn out the light.
He knows I've gone to sleep,
Therefore does not weep.
He plays with my other cat,
It could be with a rat.
He occasionally chases his tail,
But catching it, he sometimes fails.
Cleaning, the most important part of the day,
He won't do it until I look away.
He has a check up regularly,
Our vet does it monthly
He sits on my window sill,
That is till
His tea's ready,
Then he walks off steady.
At night he goes to sleep,
Without a sound but purrs deep.

Dionne Moyse (13)
Skegness Grammar School

THE ANIMATED TOWN

Holidaymakers pushing,
Business people rushing,
Small children crying,
Their mothers sighing,
Old ladies stood talking,
While dogs are out walking.
But is it ever really down,
In Skegness the busy town?

Queues about a mile long,
Please turn off that awful song,
People out to find a sale,
Oh no! I've just crushed a snail,
Hungry people munching food,
As for shopping, I'm not in the mood.
But is it ever really down,
In Skegness the busy town?

The sky is black, it's starting to rain
And these people are driving me insane,
All the umbrellas soon shoot out,
They are every colour without a doubt,
It's getting late, the people disappear,
I'm free to move now, the paths are clear,
But is it ever really down,
In Skegness the busy town?

Danica Hammond (13)
Skegness Grammar School

WINTER

Snow is falling, winds are blowing,
Children playing everywhere.
Snowballs flying, people laughing,
Fun and games without a care.
Toboggans whizzing, birds tweeting,
Taking in the cold crisp air.
Babies crying, mother's talking,
Wrapped up in their winter wear.
Cars skidding, snowman building,
People stop to watch and stare.
Frost-biting, winter whitening,
All the plants and trees are bare.

Stacey Grant (13)
Skegness Grammar School

THE CROC

There once was a considerate crocodile,
A vulture who eats between his meals,
In moving slowly he has no peer,
Camped on a tropic riverside,
He need not laugh or snigger,
He lays a great and mighty king,
No more, no less,
I am one he did not save,
A stranger approached this spot with gravity,
Under the wide and starry sky,
That only last an hour,
They're long and slender as an eel,
Dig me and let me die.

Karla Hodson (13)
The Priory, Lincoln School of Science & Technology

LOVE AND ROMANCE

Red, white, lilac and pink,
Love and romance in your heart,
But hoping every day that he is going to stay,
Will he? Won't he?
You go on wondering and repeatedly asking
Yourself every day,
Not knowing if he is going to return!

You wake up at dawn,
Is he there?
You worry if he is not home from work,
You worry if he is at the shop too long,
You're totally flummoxed!
When can you stop yourself worrying?

Love feels like a segment of your heart which
Is just based on love,
You cannot get it out of you,
When you are in love the only person which
You are bothered about is your partner.
But is he bothered about you?
Does he really care?

One day he is full of passion and buying
You bunches of roses and boxes of chocolates.
The next day he is dictative, hard-faced and
Has no feeling,
So you wonder . . .
Should my life really revolve around him?
Please . . . please think!
Then make the best decision!

Shakira Young (12)
The Priory, Lincoln School of Science & Technology

TIME

The spot on my cheek,
I look a right freak.
Big, bright and green,
Lucky I've never been seen.
I put on the spot lotion,
Huh some kind of magic potion.
Slapping it on for the first time,
Hoping that I will look fine.
Hey I am late for my date,
It's five minutes past eight.
I run to the door,
Oh no I am late now for sure.
I pull my Ford Fiesta out of the gate,
Look at the time it's ten-past eight.
The clock ticking on, will I have time?
Why did I ever make this poem rhyme?

Liam Creane (12)
The Priory, Lincoln School of Science & Technology

WHAT DOES CHRISTMAS MEAN TO YOU?

C   hrist was born,
H   ay in the manger where He was born,
R   isen at Easter,
I   srael was where He travelled to,
S   tars were shining bright for the Wise Men to follow,
T   rees to celebrate,
M   essages from the angels,
A   ndrew was one of His disciples,
S   aviour for the world.

Thomas Hart (12)
The Priory, Lincoln School of Science & Technology

THE WOLF

The wolf, a silent beauty of the night,
Its silver, glistening fur shines in the moonlight,
Like a silver coin in a dark pond.

So kind so gentle?

It moves to the dark, everything is still,
It sinks its teeth into the deep palms of death
As it furiously devours its prey.

A born killer!

So sweet or is it?

Debbie Hubbard (12)
The Priory, Lincoln School of Science & Technology

LIFE

My vision is blurred,
As I open my eyes,
Nothing can I see,
As days pass and weeks go by,
My vision gets better,
My memory develops,
More years and more weeks,
I'm getting older.
They say life begins at 40.
What have I done with my life?
I've now reached 80, my eyesight's going.
Oh, God, what have I been doing?

Nicholas Blakesley (12)
The Priory, Lincoln School of Science & Technology

AUTUMN

I wake up after a frosty
Night, autumn's here,
With crunchy leaves
As I walk through them to school.

With my warm coat, hat and gloves,
The trees are bare.

With conker fights in the playground
People can't wait until Hallowe'en,
Autumn after school,
Hot cups of tea and stew.

As autumn ends we will all
Gather round a bonfire
It's my favourite time of
The year.

Graeme Greenwood (12)
The Priory, Lincoln School of Science & Technology

SYDNEY

Did you see it?
Wasn't it great?
For four years we had to wait
All the training
And hard work,
They must have been nervous
But it was worth it,
11 medals we won,
We'll be back in Athens,
In the next four years,
Doing better than ever.

Scott Machin (12)
The Priory, Lincoln School of Science & Technology

What Is A Million

What is a million?

All the pebbles on the beach,
All the things you cannot reach.

All the droplets in an April shower,
All the times you water a flower.

All the clouds in the sky,
All the times you want to cry.

All the times you take a step,
All the times you get wet.

These are a million.

Ian Drewery (12)
The Priory, Lincoln School of Science & Technology

Life

Life is just a meaningless line of stages,
Baby, infant, student, teenager, adult,
Grandparent and then death!

What is the meaning of our existence?
Did we want to be born into this mad
And upsetting world?

Did we really want to cry when we did?
Is it right to upset people for no reason?
Did we really want to be enemies and
Die without making friends?

Gemma Goymer (13)
The Priory, Lincoln School of Science & Technology

Do This, Do That

Do this, do that,
Tidy your room, keep it clean,
Mum says to me.

Get your homework done,
Or you can't go out,
Eat all your tea or no pudding.

No you can't have it, is all I'm told,
It's for your own good,
You have to learn.

Is being a teen always like this? No!
At least my name has changed a little
Silly Sally I used to be.

Growing up is fun and hard,
Playing and learning at the same time,
Work gets harder as the school gets bigger.

Preparing me for becoming an
Adult!

Sally Austen (12)
The Priory, Lincoln School of Science & Technology

The Games

The plane lands at Sydney Airport,
I get off, the press and fans are there,
I head for the carts, go to the hotel
But then more press and fans are blocking my way.

I finally get in the car and head to the hotel,
On the way I see the stadium,
The big white building standing tall waiting
For me to show them all!

After training I head to bed
Because tomorrow is the big day
I get to sleep really excited
Because tomorrow isn't far away.

I am in the stadium ready for action,
I am doing badminton with my mate,
We finish, we won and we are in,
The next round, hip hip hooray!

Scott Flynn (12)
The Priory, Lincoln School of Science & Technology

A LETTER TO MUM

You always seem to be right there
Standing by my side
Sometimes we don't even talk
Or see eye to eye
But we always start talking again
When I want my dinner!
I don't know what I'd do without you
You always seem to care
My life would be upside down if you
Weren't always there
When I grow up I want to be
Just like you
You may not believe it but it's true
So now I've said all this stuff
I think it's time for you
I'm going town later
And I need ten pounds to spend!

Joanne Clay (12)
The Priory, Lincoln School of Science & Technology

MY GRANDAD

My grandad is a smily man,
always happy and grinning.
he laughs at himself,
but I love him because
he's my grinning grandad.

My granddad is a tubby man,
his tummy is round and plump.
When he cuddles you, you get squashed,
but I don't mind because . . .
he's my tubby grandad.

My grandad is a content man,
he never asks for more,
he insists he does everything himself,
and I'm so proud of him because
he's my content grandad.

My granddad is the best,
I'm so lucky to have him,
but no one could beat
this perfect man.
My big old grandad.

PS He's Mine!

Natasha Reidie (12)
The Priory, Lincoln School of Science & Technology

IF

If I was a bird, I would fly away high,
If I was a snail, I would hide in my shell,
If I was a worm, I would bury underground,
If I was a giraffe, I would hide near a tree,
But be careful people might see!

If only I was a bird, I could fly from my problems,
If only I was a snail, I could hide in my shell and nobody could see me,
If only I was a worm, I would bury underground,
If only I was a giraffe, I would scare people away,
But at the moment, I don't care what people say!

Charlotte Baynton (12)
The Priory, Lincoln School of Science & Technology

I HATE GOING TO SCHOOL

'Should I go to school today?'

Food that smells like rotten eggs.
The children shouting as loud as they can,
They give me terrible headaches!

But there is my very good friend,
She is so kind to me and at the end
Of the day I do get paid.

There is that cat, I love it so,
I feed it every day,
But it makes me mad when
Horrid boys scare it away.

There is that gorgeous teacher,
He just strolls by but he gives me evil looks,
Which make me want to cry.

'I think I'll go to school today,
I've got no reason to stay,
Apart from half of the things above,
OK I think I'll stay at home.'

I hate being a dinner lady!

Fiona Maxwell (12)
The Priory, Lincoln School of Science & Technology

WHAT IS CHRISTMAS?

What
Is this
Thing that is
Happening soon?
Is it a person, an object
Or a thing? Does it hurt you in
The night while you're sleeping?
Is it like a tornado furiously whipping
And whirling around our village? Are you
Just meant to stand and observe? Does every
Single person take part?
Is it a
Merry time?
Will I ever
Experience
Christmas?

Kelly Richardson (12)
The Priory, Lincoln School of Science & Technology

LOVE IS . . .

Caring about all around you.
Sharing with each other the happy and sad times.
Considering their feelings at all times.
Understanding that all around are different,
Accepting and appreciating them for who
And what they are.
Supporting them when they are in need,
Having enough love to forgive.

Liam Linch (12)
The Priory, Lincoln School of Science & Technology

MY BROTHER

He's always here, he's always there,
And that's what bothers me
I need some time, I need some space
I need to be alone
If he could give me five minutes
Just alone, just me
Then I would love him twice as much
And I would be happy.

When I'm walking down the street
Maybe to buy some bread
He follows me
On every twist and turn
If he could give me five minutes
Just alone, just me
Then I would love him twice as much
And I would be happy.

Ben Jablonski (12)
The Priory, Lincoln School of Science & Technology

DRIVEN

Deep in the sombre potholes of the diabolical underworld,
Judas shrieks in wrath audible even on Earth,
Doesn't he always,
I mean, make an influence in our lives,
As if we're puppets and he's our master.

Marc Garner (13)
The Priory, Lincoln School of Science & Technology

CHRISTMAS

Christmas
What do you think?
Well I think it is really great
Yes it is the best time of the year
But,
What is it for?
You may think it is just for presents,
But it is mainly for the presents, but
I bet
You feel like jumping with joy
But yes OK, that is very true,
Christmastime is brilliant
Think
Not only presents
But all about happiness,
Christmas is all about being thankful
Forgive
Forgive the people,
Who are forgetting you
But always remember it is a way of
Saying thank you!

Victoria Burnett (12)
The Priory, Lincoln School of Science & Technology

AUTUMN

One misty autumn morning
I saw some murky fog
As I gazed out of my window
And stroked my beloved dog.

When I went outside I got a big surprise
I looked down beneath my feet and couldn't believe my eyes
There I saw beneath my feet brown leaves glistening in the dew
And in the sky the sun shone down with a dull orange hue.

Bonfire Night's not far away
Come on guys, come out to play,
Get the sticks, come this way
Light the fire and watch the display.

Kathryn Guest (12)
The Priory, Lincoln School of Science & Technology

MY DAD'S BIRTHDAY PRESENT

I have a dad who is really a pain
Because when it's his birthday
We say 'not again'.

We wrack our brains in despair
As he has everything,
But he likes fresh air.

Although he's a nuisance
And although he's a pain
We decided to send him on a plane.

He sat in the pilot's seat
With his headphones on.
He revved up the engine, and then he was gone.

We were very proud of him
As he flew in the sky.
We could not see him, when he flew up high.

After an hour it was time to come back
He is so happy now he's got the knack.
Now we know and won't despair, because every birthday
He can go in the air!

Luke Billett (12)
The Priory, Lincoln School of Science & Technology

WHAT IS A TEENAGER?

A teenager is someone who can stay up late,
and someone who can get into really scary movies,
but a teenager is someone who goes to bed late and can't get up in
the morning and turns into a great big scary monster
with spots
and wild hair.
But a teenager is someone who gets respected (or else!)
and if they're not, then tough!
A teenager is someone who has Kevin Patterson as an idol.
But a teenager is someone who hates exams.
A teenager is someone who can't be called a kid
unless they act like one!
A teenager is someone who has clothes like a tramp
and a face like a dalmation.
That is what a teenager is!

Kayleigh Stringer (12)
The Priory, Lincoln School of Science & Technology

MY MUM

My mum is not a normal mum
Her favourite fruit is definitely plum
All she does is cook-n-clean,
But I think she's a washing machine.

My mum's favourite sport is bed making
But when she asks me to, I start a-shaking
I call her mum-o-mantic
But she really is an exercise fanatic.

My mum means a lot to me
'Cause she is part of our mad family.

Matthew Ford (12)
The Priory, Lincoln School of Science & Technology

PETROL

No petrol here, no petrol there
No blummin' petrol anywhere.
London's as bare as Antarctica.
Cardiff's as dry as a desert.
No petrol here, no petrol there,
No blummin' petrol anywhere.

No petrol here, no petrol there,
No blummin' petrol anywhere.
Volvo's run out, Mercedes none.
There's lot of petrol, where's it gone?
No petrol here, no petrol there,
No blummin' petrol anywhere.

No petrol here, no petrol there,
No blummin' petrol anywhere.
It started in France, those stupid frogs.
No LRP to work your cogs.
No petrol here, no petrol there,
No blummin' petrol anywhere.

No petrol here, no petrol there
No blummin' petrol anywhere,
They nicked our milk, they stole our bread.
Our cars are hungry they need to be fed.
No petrol here, no petrol there,
No blummin' petrol anywhere.

Christopher Griffiths (12)
The Priory, Lincoln School of Science & Technology

UNCAGED

It was cold in there, dark as well and I dreaded that
Same time every day when they would come and get me.
The pain some days became unbearable and there was a
Constant ringing in my ears from that fateful day.

I hated being there, away from my mother and the ones
Close to me. Why was I chosen to live this destiny?
When I first came there was a row of empty cages which
Soon became full with angry, fearful animals like myself,
Getting more and more confused the longer they were kept here.

Their pale hands were freezing cold and grasped my
Soft fur with unkind fingers, it was worse this time as
There were more people with white coats and gloves,
A needle moved toward me and then . . .

Helen-Louise Moss (12)
The Priory, Lincoln School of Science & Technology

TEENAGE THOUGHTS

At times I wish I was on a different planet
With nobody there not a care in the world!
Adults think you are a child when really it's just in their head.

Adults are just pretend, they're not really there.
Always moaning, always groaning, they think they
Always know best but most of the time they are
Wrong anyway.

'Don't daydream, don't this, don't do that.'
They just go on and on,
Don't care about my feelings,
That's just the way adults are I suppose!

Rebecca Hammerton (12)
The Priory, Lincoln School of Science & Technology

SARCASTIC SENTENCES ABOUT SCHOOL

S   chool's great
C   an't fault school
H   ow come we can't go to school at weekends?
O   ld people should come to school
O   ne hour long homework would be fun
L   earning's as fun as being on the fastest roller-coaster in the world.

I   nteresting lessons
S   chool is like Heaven

G   ood thorough lessons
R   eading for hours is ace
E   veryone should enjoy school
A   t 3.05 when we go home for the weekend I cry
T   omorrow should be a school day.

Scott Tysoe (12)
The Priory, Lincoln School of Science & Technology

DREAMING

When I dream, I feel like I enter another world,
A parallel world that you drop into as you fall asleep.
You are capable of anything . . . everything can happen,
You can become a fighter pilot or be chased by zombies.
Another dimension is unleashed into your mind.
I have been to the underworld and back . . . all in a dream.
It always feels so real, yet so unreal . . .
Sometimes I feel like I have endured a ten storey drop
From a skyscraper and yet lived on.
I may fall out of a helicopter or even become a martial arts' master,
Falling off a cliff and wake up just before I hit the ground . . .
It can all happen, only in a dream.

Dominic Finch (12)
The Priory, Lincoln School of Science & Technology

THE MACHINE

As he rumbled over the hill,
As he waded through swamps,
As he swallowed up forests,
As he spread his black breath.

The hills groaned under his weight,
The swamps parted in his wake,
The forest trembled at his feet,
The clouds inhaled his poisonous murmur.

As he deafened surrounding wildlife,
As he murdered innocent lives,
As his smoky gas engulfed all plants,
As he powerfully commanded nature.

The wildlife covered their delicate ears,
The lives were wasted and destroyed,
The plants choked and coughed,
The nature bowed to him.

As he slowed and stopped,
As he got dragged away,
As he was crushed and burned,
As he was melted and reborn.

The forests rejoiced and sang,
The hills relaxed their backs,
The swamps bubbled with happiness,
The nature prepared for a new dark reign.

Adam McGrath (12)
The Priory, Lincoln School of Science & Technology

SCHOOL DINNERS!

School dinners are great.
School dinners are wicked.
School dinners, everyone should
Have them at school.
I'm a dinner lady at this school.

Ahh! When you smell it, it's like
Lovely smooth silky chocolate, but
By the time you've rushed to the canteen.
Got to the end of the queue,
They've all sold out of hot dogs, chips
And your favourite, but sometimes manky
Cookies.
But they're nice though, kind of.
I'm a pupil at this school.

I don't like clearing up after all the
Students in the canteen.
Clearing up the half-eaten chips,
The trodden in burgers, you know.
That really annoys me.
Especially those kids in the corner they think
They're so smart, they do.
By accidentally dropping some chips onto the
Floor and flicking peas, well that's what they say,
'It was by accident.'
Well that wouldn't have happened in
My
Day . . .

Chris Monslow (12)
The Priory, Lincoln School of Science & Technology

BIRTH TO DEATH

You feel the push
And you hurtle yourself out like a bullet from a gun.
You're the size of a board rubber,
Your new life has begun.

You reach the age of three,
You can say a lot of words by now,
You start to walk around the world,
Seeing lots of new things.

You're much older by now,
Beginning to get to know the feeling of life,
Not knowing what's around the corner,
You start to think, 'Where am I going in life and when will I die?'

Good or bad, you are a teenager,
You have your first kiss behind the bike sheds,
Spots appear and you hate yourself,
You're growing up fast, as quick as a sunflower at full growth.

You become eighteen, you're an adult,
You can drive and drink and you're still free,
You decide to leave home,
Your mum worries and your dad feels proud.
You get wed to the right girl and have children,
Dreading what they will turn out like.

You're getting old,
Becoming a grandma or grandad,
Enjoying the rest of life while it lasts,
And collecting your pension every week.

The time comes, you take one last look at the world,
All your happy memories crowded into your head like
100 people on a No. 42 bus,
Then you're finished, you life is no more!

James Igoea (13)
The Priory, Lincoln School of Science & Technology

THE LONER

Why are friends never right
In personality?
Why am I the only one
Who can never see?

What do I have to do
And do I have to try
To get someone to like me?
Do I have to lie?

And if I do, what do I say?
Do I laugh and smile?
Do I show the real me?
Or hide me in denial?

If only I knew the answer,
Maybe I'd have some friends.
Instead of being a loner,
My loneliness would end.

Freya Morgan (12)
The Priory, Lincoln School of Science & Technology

MY MATE

My mate, she's great
She's got . . .

Hair like a lions
But she's as gentle as a kitten,
Feet as tough as leather
But skin as soft as snow.

Teeth like rabbits
But she doesn't bite,
Eyes as blue as water
But she hates swimming.

A body like elastic
But she's no good at gym,
Skin as dark as the night
But she shines like the sun.

My mate, she's great
But she's only imaginary.

Sarah McCay (12)
The Priory, Lincoln School of Science & Technology

CHILDREN AND TEACHERS

Those silly kids
Why are they always talking like that?
Chatter, chatter,
The only thing they do is chatter.

Us children,
We're not silly, we never talk,
The teachers maybe think we're talking,
But we're never quiet, like a butterfly.

Those silly kids,
They never hand in their homework on time,
Sorry Miss I forgot it,
They say the same excuses every time.

Us children,
We always hand our homework in on time,
It's never sorry Miss I forgot it,
We're as good as angels.

Joseph Ogden (12)
The Priory, Lincoln School of Science & Technology

A WOUND UP SANTA

I
Really
Really
Don't like
Christmas
At all very much
When I get ready and start to think,
All those thoughts come rushing back and make me pink.
'I want this, I want that,' and 'He's getting one!'
But, the answer is now going to be,
No   No
No   No
But come that very, very sweet day,
When I jump and ride upon my sleigh
The cold night air flushes all my stresses away!

Sam Phillips (13)
The Priory, Lincoln School of Science & Technology

THE SOLDIER

The wind blew over grassy meadows,
Of Northern France
And harmony was shattered,
By the dugout trenches,
Whilst the men got ready for war.

They stand ready to fight
Guns poised,
But deep down inside,
None of them wanted,
To do it at all.

The pining and heartache,
Was overwhelming,
As all of them,
Remembering
Their families at home.

The soldier ran out blind with emotion
And the cry pierced every heart,
As he had fallen,
A life shattered
And lost.

The next morning,
The mourners came,
Depressed families,
Weeped in each other's arms,
As all I could do was look around and say
Rest in peace my friend,
Rest in peace
As I stand in this destroyed, chaotic place.

Laura McDonald (12)
The Priory, Lincoln School of Science & Technology

LIFE OF A FLY

Fly born from an egg
Fly flying freely in his carefree world
Fly happy as a newborn baby
Fly living as long as you or me
Zapp!
Fly life cut short by the bug zapper.

Chris Paton (12)
The Priory, Lincoln School of Science & Technology

FRIENDS

I met a family on holiday,
We had happy times and sad,
Our days were filled with sunshine,
We were nearly always happy and glad.

We sunned ourselves around the pool,
Had lovely family times together,
All our worries washed away,
Oh I wish it could have lasted forever.

It came the day, when we did depart,
I really thought it would break our hearts,
But I'm sure we'll meet again someday.
I hope our friendship will outlive our stay.

Travelling again we hope to be,
Over the sea to their country,
Sharing all our memories which are so true,
And living life to the full, both me and you.

Melanie Gatenby (12)
The Robert Manning Technology College

ANIMAL POEM

I love pigeons
I love dogs
I love rabbits
And also frogs

I don't like butterflies
I don't like bats
I don't like moths
And I don't like rats

I like cats
I like pigs
I like hamsters
And I like earwigs

I hate ladybirds
I hate snails
I hate butterflies
And whales

I don't mind flies
I don't mind bears
I don't mind cows
And I don't mind hares.

Kerry Croft (12)
The Robert Manning Technology College

A POEM BY LIAM GALLAGHER!

The day I went to Rutland Zoo,
I saw a bouncing kangaroo,
Big ears, a big nose,
But you couldn't miss his massive toes!

As I walked through the park,
I saw the rare white shark,
I sat down and had a rest,
I even took off my woollen vest.

So the end of another cracking day,
School tomorrow, wahay!

Liam Gallagher (11)
The Robert Manning Technology College

THE ZOMBIES ARE COMING

When they walk they stomp
When they eat they chomp
Their talk is ghostly
I think they do it to warn me
The zombies are coming

They walk but they're dead
They carry their head
They make loads of noise
I think it's to warn boys
The zombies are coming

Their legs are stiff
They're not just a myth
They talk in shrills
I think they're warning girls
The zombies are coming

They can't jump about
They can't even shout
They talk about kill
I think they will warn us
The zombies are coming.

Ben Turner (12)
The Robert Manning Technology College

HOLIDAY MEMORIES

Holidays are always fun,
Especially when we're in the sun,
France is where I like to go,
But not to the Alps
With the freezing snow.

Down in the west where the surf rolls in,
Miles of golden beach for the eyes to take in,
Crest of the waves fall at my feet,
Prickling of my skin from the intense summer heat.

Pavement cafes are bustling with chatter,
Coffee, croissant or pain au chocolat.
I like moules and frites for my supper
But when I get home it's back to bread and butter.

As I drive home I remember the good times
I've had with me and my brother,
My mum and my dad.

Rachel Palmer (11)
The Robert Manning Technology College

MY POEM ABOUT MONEY

Money, money it's all around us,
It doesn't grow on trees,
It grows in banks.

Money, money, it's hard to get,
You can't grow it,
You've got to save it.

Felicity Fisher (12)
The Robert Manning Technology College

FRONT TO BACK

There was a time when the cat barked and the dog purred,
Doesn't this sound so absurd,
There was a time when the fish flew and the bird swam
When the ostrich slithered and the snail ran.

There was a time when we played at night and slept in the day,
When the summer was November and winter was May,
There was a time when lemons were sweet,
When gloves were worn upon your feet,

There was a time when lightning banged and thunder flashed,
When cymbals honked,
And horns clashed.

There was a time when sky was green and grass was blue,
When you were I and I was you,

Why do we make our lives so complicated?
Maybe I'd have a better poem if I'd waited.

Sophie Russell (11)
The Robert Manning Technology College

DINOSAUR

D   inos everywhere, can't get away.
I   n you hair, everywhere.
N   o one can scare a big dinosaur.
O   n the land there's footprints to show.
S   ee the dinos as they shake the ground.
A   crowd of dinos is charging towards you.
U   nlike the land animals there's sea life too.
R   ound the water they swim to cool down.

Oliver Abrams (12)
The Robert Manning Technology College

BIRTHDAY

Another year has nearly gone,
A few more hours,
It won't be long,
Last year I got a football kit,
Some CDs and some money.
A few other things have slipped my mind now, that's funny.
I think I gave enough of the clues,
About what I'd really like,
Number one on my list,
Was a silver BMX bike.
I'd ride around and do some tricks,
And when I'd mastered the difficult bits,
I'd race over to my friend's house,
And show him what I can do.
But hold on, what if the message didn't get through!
And I've got a load of presents,
That I didn't really want.
I will have to wait until Christmas then,
Which is months and months away.
But hold on don't panic,
The time has come to see
Whether a BMX bike is for me.
I hope it's the right colour,
And has got stunt pegs,
Please let it be the best present forever and ever.

Kevin Elger (11)
The Robert Manning Technology College

WHY?

Why go to school,
When you could be going to the swimming pool?
Why have to work at the age of 13?
Especially if you have been forced to fix a machine.
Why have to work for money?
I really don't find that funny.
Why learn to be responsible that's what mums are for,
Like on the way out of the house we have to close the door.
Why waste time to read and write,
And also learning to eat and fight?
Why wash up dirty plates?
Buy a dishwasher, listen to my mates.
Why do homework? We get enough at school,
If you're the one who invented it you are definitely a fool.
Why read books when you have a TV?
Watch TV and be like me.
Why make my own tea,
It should already be there waiting for me.
Why do education? We have better things to do,
Like going to a theme park or having a taboo
Why do anything? I'm sure we'd like to know,
But I bet if we ask you something you'll probably say no.
We really should work because that's what life's about,
Otherwise you would be lazy and have no energy to shout.
Not everything has a reason why,
So anyway I have to go, c'ya, whenever, bye!

Tara Delf (13)
The Robert Manning Technology College

BASKETBALL

B asketball is fast and furious and very fun
A nd it's something that is rising fast in the UK.
S urprisingly you can play even if you have ever played in your life.
K een or not, it is still fun.
E ven people who have never played it before still enjoy.
T he great thing about it is people don't take it as serious as other sports.
B oth girls and boys can play it too, which is great.
A nd all ages too.
L earning how to play is easy.
L anky basketball players.

Thomas Fuller (11)
The Robert Manning Technology College

A POEM ALL ABOUT ME

Me I have two cheeks,
Me I have two hands,
Me I have eight fingers,
Which help me play in bands!

Me I have two ears,
Me I have two eyes,
Me I have one pair of glasses,
Which help me see when I buy!

Me I have two feet,
Me I have two arms,
Me I have two palms,
Which help me set off alarms.

Vicki Bennett (13)
The Robert Manning Technology College

THE BIG CHANGE

It was the change I didn't want to make,
I was a bag of nerves, it made me shake.
When I got up it was bad,
Very bad.
I was forced to get into the car
The day wasn't going according to par.
I got there feeling sad
But in the end I was glad because it wasn't so bad.
The first bit was nothing
The second bit, I was laughing.
The canteen was quite tasty
But, was I being too hasty?
The afternoon went a bit slow
I was waiting for the bell to let us go.
What a busy day I had
Secondary school wasn't so bad!

Daniel Chalmers (12)
The Robert Manning Technology College

AT THE RACE

You can go fast or slow,
First, second, third,
Now round the chicane we go,
Round the first bend, then round the next,
Twisting, turning, side to side,
Then down the home straight,
Car on the left, car on the right,
Car behind, car in front,
Nowhere to go.

Andrew Whyte (12)
The Robert Manning Technology College

MY MUM

My mum, my mum
How horrid she can be
She moans and moans to make me eat me tea,
She's already killed my brother and now she's after me.

I don't know what to do with her
I don't know what to say
I think she's going mental and my dad has gone away.

Someone come and help me quick
She's seen me
She's found me, what shall I do?
Run, hide
I haven't got a clue.

Antony Crane (12)
The Robert Manning Technology College

HOMEWORK

Why do we have homework?
What is it for?
We already do enough in class
Why give us anymore?

We try hard in the lessons
I think we deserve a rest
They give us so much to do
To be honest I think they're pests.

I've heard the lectures
And I think they're poor
'You need to try your very best'
But what for?

Abby Sommers (12)
The Robert Manning Technology College

A BIRD'S LIFE

I look around,
and I have found
that life has just begun,
the sky is blue
and out I flew
from the birth of my dear home.

I saw trees and looked around
I saw the houses on the ground
I heard my mother calling me,
so off I flew back to my tree.

My nest is snug
warm and soft
my brothers and sisters fly aloft.

My mother has now fed me,
so now I can go and see
my brothers and sisters who are playing
around an old oak tree.

Now the night is drawing
the day is coming to a close,
I go back to my home
I sleep the whole night through
not feeling at all alone.

So now you know my life as a bird,
I have just now spoken my very first word!

Ashleigh Westbrook (13)
The Robert Manning Technology College

WHERE WOULD WE BE WITHOUT BOYS?

The world is full of boys,
You love them or hate them,
And sometimes you date them,

Where would we be without boys?

They strut around school,
And think they're real cool,
With their hair full of gel,
And their peculiar smell,

Where would we be without boys?

They play boyish games,
Like football and pool,
Over Britney and Buffy,
They all drool,

We all love you really boys!

Jade Siciliano (13)
The Robert Manning Technology College

TOGETHER POEM

Together we have happiness,
Passion and romance,
Your gentle love is like a flame,
Burning in my heart.

The sun is warm and peaceful,
Like your soothing thoughts,
When sunrise comes,
We have some fun,
Playing in the garden.

The seasons gracefully flowing through,
One by one they come and go,
The fine heat, the swift wind,
All remind me of you!

Ellen Burrows (11)
The Robert Manning Technology College

CHOCOLATE

Chocolate is my favourite food,
I eat it when I'm in the mood.
It stimulates the tongue and brain,
And makes me happy when I'm sane.

It stops my craving and helps me think,
Will this chocolate make me stink?
Some chocolates are for desserts,
And some are for the boring adverts.

Sometimes chocolate is really rich,
It's for those matches on the pitch.
Goes on crumpets, goes on toast,
That's why I love it the most.

Chocolate is in gateaux and cake,
Which I always love to make.
When I eat that chocolate cake,
It gives me a bad stomach ache.

But at the end of this long day,
All I say is I love . . .
Chocolate!

Sabrina Booth (12)
The Robert Manning Technology College

A POEM ABOUT ME

I am a very loyal friend,
My keenness for music will never end,
Other things I do and enjoy,
Make me a sporty type of boy.

I'm caring and I'm honest,
That's the side of me I like,
Yet when I'm naughty and cheeky,
I become a little tyke.

Science and DT are my strengths,
To achieve in them I go to great lengths,
At this school I'll do my best,
Not just with science but in all the rest.

My mother and father they always love me,
But the silly thing is that I never see,
That when I have a problem or a need,
My parents are always there for me.

Stuart Kershaw (11)
The Robert Manning Technology College

POEMS

I don't like writing poems,
I don't know what to write,
The words just don't come quickly,
Oh, help me, what a sight.

I don't like writing poems,
It's not always a success,
The ink is blotting on the paper,
I'm getting in a mess.

I don't like writing poems,
I'd rather be at games,
If I get it right this time,
I could be in the hall of fames.

I don't like writing poems,
I'm waiting to be fed,
By the time I've finished this one,
I could be nearly dead.

Ryan Ellis (11)
The Robert Manning Technology College

MR NOBODY!

I know a little man,
As quiet as a mouse!
He's the one who does mischief,
In everyone's house!

He puts the damp wood on the fire,
That kettles can't boil;
His are the feet that bring in the mud,
Which makes the carpet soil!

The finger marks on the door,
Which none of us made!
We never leave the blinds unclosed,
To let the sofas' fade!

I know a little man,
As quiet as a mouse!
He's the one who does mischief
In everyone's house!

Jodie Findlay
The Robert Manning Technology College

TREES

It's a beautiful day
Leaves are falling from the trees
Reds,
Oranges,
Yellows
And browns
Crunch, crunch, crunch they go
As you squash them beneath your feet
Trees become bare
Swaying their dull empty branches
In the bitter cold air
Soon it will be winter
Then the freezing ice and snows will come
Covering the trees
In a thin glistening layer
Now it is spring
All the ice has gone
And buds appear upon the trees
The buds
Suddenly burst open
Freeing the new green leaves
All through the summer
The leaves shimmer
In the warm comforting sun
Giving shade
For the perfect picnic
But soon it will be autumn again
And all the same things
Shall happen once again.

Natalie Walker (13)
The Robert Manning Technology College

KEVIN KEEGAN

When Kevin Keegan left being manager of England,
The team was a disgrace,
The question is, who's going to take his place?

He hung up his boots at the end of the game
He was full of just, endless shame.

They were defeated by the Germans,
A disappointment he could not bear.
The burden he could not share.

Three people who want to take his place,
His pride,
In being there so they don't slide.

Abbie Ward (11)
The Robert Manning Technology College

WHAT AM I?

I send messages at top speed,
I can give any information that you may need,
I can send a letter and connect you to the Internet if you wish.

Store your friends' numbers,
Lots of ringing tones for you to choose,
Choice of networks you can have,
WAP technology, the latest fad.

What am I?

I'm a mobile phone of course!

James Kendall (11)
The Robert Manning Technology College

ANIMALS ARE SO CUTE, LIKE DOGS

A nimals are quiet,
N ot annoying,
I love them,
M akes me happy,
A nimals can be quite furry,
L ovely to have,
S tay calm all the time.

A nimals are beautiful,
R unning all over the place,
E xtremely cute.

S o nice to see,
O ut to be friendly.

C uddly and warm,
U nusual are some pets
T ime goes fast when they are there,
E xciting all the time.

L onely when they are not there,
I think all animals should be treated the same,
K ind and special,
E specially dogs.

D on't do anything bad,
O vercome by love and caring,
G o softer every day,
S o funny and lovely.

Louise Roberts (11)
The Robert Manning Technology College

GOODNIGHT MR TOM

G ood to read
O bviously Will is best friends with Zak
O uch, that hurt (he fell off the bike)
D oesn't ever want to see a psychiatrist again
N ever wants to leave Mr Tom
I nconsiderate characters like Will's mum
G reat characters
H ospitable villagers
T om Oakley becomes a dad

M um called Will blasphemer
R opes cut into Will's arms

T rudy died in Will's arms
'O h Mister Tom it's the best birthday'
M other was a person with a split personality.

Alys Baines-Dinning (12)
The Robert Manning Technology College

CAN I

Can ...
No,
I ...
No,
Go ...
Shhh ...
Out ...
Not on your ...
Please,
Don't interrupt!

Luke Lattimer-Rogers (13)
The Robert Manning Technology College

FIRST CONTACT!

When two cells meet, a new life forms,
Nine months later a baby then is born,
A result of first contact.

A mother's love, that first tender touch,
A special bond is formed.

They land on the moon, a galactic place.
Imagine the look upon their faces,
When first contact is made.

Eye to eye across a crowded room,
Two people meet, hearts flutter and boom.
First contact is made not a moment too soon.

That long lost relative not seen for years,
First contact provokes immediate tears.

A stone on stone, and fire is made,
A very primitive tool
Used by an ancient caveman,
Who never went to school.

A spark from a plug to ignite the fuel
That drives the car along,
The connection from battery to point,
That we get our torch light from.

A meteor flying through space, at speed,
Hits the Earth, a first contact we do not need!

A punch that is thrown out of despair,
A pinch on the arm, or a pull of the hair,
The pain of first contact can be so hard to bear.

A soft spoken word that shows you care,
When nobody else seems to be there.

First contact is always there.

Becky Peake (12)
The Robert Manning Technology College

I WANT

I want a wide-screen TV.
I want Sky Digital.
I want a PC.
I want a BMW.
I want a high-tec video.
I want to be a millionaire.
I want a radio-controlled car which runs on petrol.
I want to fly an aeroplane called an F-15.
I want all the PlayStation games.
I want a Walkman.
I want a hi-fi system.
I want a motorbike.
I want a quadbike.
I want an off-road motorbike.
I want a Nighthawk.
I want a Scalextric.
I want a Game Boy.
I want a Nintendo 64.
I want everything in the world
But what I want I cannot have!

Steven Taylor (11)
The Robert Manning Technology College

SEASONS

In *spring*
The buds on the trees getting ready to grow,
They are giving off a very bright glow.

In *summer*
Golden sands gleaming in the hot summer sun,
Children in the park having lots of fun.

In *autumn*
Autumn leaves falling to the ground,
Walking through them big crunching sounds.

In *winter*
Children making snowmen in the white snow,
Snowflakes falling to the ground very slow.

The four seasons start all over again.
With a new year,
A new month,
A new week,
And a new day.

Sarah Roberts (11)
The Robert Manning Technology College

DON'T MAKE ME GO TO SCHOOL TODAY MUM!

Don't make me go to school today Mum, I feel ill.
I would rather stay at home with you today Mum.
I could play with Bill.

I would be a big help to you Mum, it's shopping day.
Don't make me go to school today Mum.
I did really well and got top marks in my spelling test yesterday.

I will look after the baby, and I've already missed the bus.
It's a teacher training day Mum.
Or how about me doing a bit of painting
Or even cutting the hedge.

Mum where are you taking me in such a hurry,
Oh Mum, you're taking me to school!

Amy Cliffe (11)
The Robert Manning Technology College

I WISH

I wish I was a bird so I could fly high into the sky,
Have wings that spread across the clouds.

I wish I was a horse so I could gallop through the country,
Have long wavy hair that blows back when I run.

I wish I was a dog, have walks three times a day,
Have fun with my owner and play every day.

I wish I was a tree, stand tall from the ground,
Grow my leaves and grow my branches.
Then grow so tall I reach the sky.

I wish I was the moon that rotates around the Earth,
To see all the planets like Jupiter and Mars.

I wish I was my mum so I could see how she copes,
To do people's hair and to cook the tea.

But what I really wish the most is for me to stay the same.

Katey Charlton (11)
The Robert Manning Technology College

A PET POEM

It was really hard to think of a poem,
I was watching my fish and then I got going!
I could do about fish, I thought suddenly,
They are dumb and stupid, this will be funny!
Then, what about that, I could write about my cat!
Then again, he ate the washing machine, now he is all fat!
Hey, what about my new hamster Mini,
She just got her new rubber dinghy!
Oh I forgot it popped in two weeks,
She was really sad, I had to buy her loads of sweets!
I got some new stick insects, they're really cool!
I found most of them walking round my school!
It's getting dark, look there's a bat, weeeee!
Oh no, ouch, he just hit a tree!
Look! Look! Shhhhh . . . It's a toad,
Oh no, a car flattened it right on the road!
I hope my cat does not try and cross the road!
I don't want him ending up flat like the toad!
He is really, really fat!
He would be much safer sleeping on the mat!
Now my cat has just gone on a fast spin,
Now he wishes he hadn't eaten that thing!
Oh well I did not think of a poem
Now I really must be going!

Sam Berry (11)
The Robert Manning Technology College

MY HAMSTER

My hamster lives in a large cage,
The bars are silver, the bottom is beige,
My hamster cage is three storeys high,
But my house is only two storeys, why?

I take him out and put him in his ball,
The way he rolls around is cool,
He sleeps through the day, and is awake at night,
He sometimes gives me quite a fright!

Kylie Pope (12)
The Robert Manning Technology College

THE PERFECT BIRTHDAY

Wake up, it's 7 o'clock
Rushing down the stairs hoping for lots of presents.
I've opened my presents
There's everything I wanted.
My own clarinet, a mobile phone, a new set of clothes
Money from my grandparents.
But no time to try them
I've got to help my mum with the party.
I've made the jelly
While Mum's making sandwiches and setting the table.
I'm going to sneak out and use my new phone.
Everything is going smoothly, everyone is coming.
Now, it's just the food that I'm waiting for.
Mum says 'Go and get dressed while I make the rest.'
My friends will be here soon, I quickly put my dress on.
We're just putting the last bits of food on the table.
Here comes all my friends.
More presents from them.
The party is great.

Laura Perry (11)
The Robert Manning Technology College

THE PAINTER

Fine brush strokes lick the paper,
With different shades of colour he paints a garden,
Which is nowhere to be found,
It is the garden of his imagination.
He sits there quietly, listening, thinking.
Greys and whites make the fine detailed colouring of the rocks.
He sits and listens to the trickling water,
The sound which he himself cannot paint.
Crimson, orange and gold leaves float on the trickling water,
They have parted from their autumn tree.
Reds, blues and purples make the vigorous colourings of the plants.
Lily pads float on the water,
With their pastel shades of pink and white.
The painting is complete.

Laura Davies (11)
The Robert Manning Technology College

ROSES ARE RED

Roses are red
Violets are blue
Let's get together
And I'll stick with you.

Roses are red
Violets are blue
Let's get together
Because I love you.

Roses are red
Violets are blue
Let's get together
Because I think you are so cool.

Kelly Bell (11)
The Robert Manning Technology College

MONKEY BOY

Monkey Boy lazes in bed,
Monkey Boy pinches my bread,
Monkey Boy hates a bath,
Monkey Boy doesn't do his homework,
Monkey Boy doesn't eat his veg,
Monkey Boy's room is a tip!

Monkey Boy lies in the sun,
Monkey Boy can't run,
Monkey Boy smells horrible,
Monkey Boy climbs trees,
Monkey Boy eats like a vulture,
Monkey Boy can't stop scratching,
But I love Monkey Boy,
Monkey Boy is my brother.

Jamie Gough (11)
The Robert Manning Technology College

POEM

It was a sunny day.
I had three jumps to go.
I'd done it!
I'd cleared the two jumps.
I was about to jump my third hurdle.
My heart was pounding.
I took a deep breath.
I had cleared it!
I got first position.
I was so proud, first place!

Hayley Bird (14)
The Robert Manning Technology College

THE OLYMPIC GAMES

At home I've seen the Olympic Games,
Watched sportsmen with their faces strained,
Athletes from around the world do their best,
Pushing, pulling and sweating to pass the test,
Running, rowing, boxing and swimming too,
Great Britain's team we're so proud of you!
Olympians great, Olympians small,
Everyone there was on the ball.
Shooting, cycling, great stories to be told,
How years of practice come through to win gold,
I think Britain came out on top,
Everyone here was like a bottle of pop!
Waving and cheering, fireworks galore,
Sydney Games 2000 were the best of all,
Sunshine, showers and drizzle too,
Didn't dampen the support for you,
Now all the athletes are on the mend,
The Sydney games have come to an end,
The ending ceremony was fantastic,
With fireworks flashing just like magic!

Emma Robinson (11)
The Robert Manning Technology College

THE BIKE RIDER

There was a young teacher from Dyke
Who loved to ride his bike
He fell in a ditch and met a witch
Who turned him into a pike.

Thomas Dixon (11)
The Robert Manning Technology College

LET THE SHOW BEGIN

Pony tails and pig tails,
Buns and plaits,
Keeping all our hair slicked tightly back.
Character, split soles,
Points and taps,
These are shoes we must not lose.
Trilbys, canes, tutus and bowers that we wear.
Pastels and pink,
Black and bolds, reds and yellows, silvers and golds,
These are the colours that make us glow,
And now to the show,
Swan Lake, Riverdance, Grease and Summer Holiday.
Soft and gentle, loud and fast,
That's the sound of the music which gives our feet the beat.
Point those toes, clip those taps,
Grab a partner and twist again.
Ballet, tap, rock and roll and jazz
A never-ending razzmatazz.

Emily Baker (12)
The Robert Manning Technology College

WATER

W ispy, washy, wet and wonderful
A ll summer down at the pool
T ry to swim in this liquidised fun
E xciting
R eally refreshing to drink

Aicha Issaoui (12)
The Robert Manning Technology College

THE FISH

I like to fish on the riverbank
It's so still and quiet
The birds fly by so silently
And the reeds blow gently in the wind

The ripples on the water
Let me know there's a fish around
The dragonflies go quickly by
I hope I soon get a fish

I sit with my rod across the water
My float is bobbing up and down
There is a fish somewhere in there
But I'll have to be more patient

Some cows walk by in a line
Chewing the grass as they go along
They seem a bit frightened of me
But I'm only there for the fish

I can see a heron in the distance
He'll be looking for food
But it won't come near me and my fish
In a flash he takes off and flies away

A fresh piece of bait is what I need
To make the fish come closer
Still I sit on the riverbank
Just waiting, hoping

It's getting dark now and I'll soon have to go
But just a bit longer, it's worth the wait
A barn owl flutters by
But I'll get that fish very soon

And then my float goes under
A tug on the line and yes, I've got one
Gently pulling it in, I land it safely,
A big beautiful carp.

Ben Cooke (11)
The Robert Manning Technology College

WITCHES

On their brooms,
Flying high,
Through the skies,
Making trouble,
On the double.

They fly over the houses,
Causing trouble,
Hiss, boom and bubble,
That's the ways,
Of their trouble.

Black cats,
Pointy hats,
Magic brooms,
Cauldron of dooms.

Wicca is their religion,
Spell book is their bible,
Black cats in the legends,
Hallowe'en is the time
For bewitching,
Full moons you might be itching.

So to all of you out on a full moon . . . Beware!

Faye Stockdale (11)
The Robert Manning Technology College

The Cat

I went for a walk the other week,
When suddenly, I heard a shriek,
On turning round I saw a stray
And began to head that way.

The cat was very cold and wet,
Thrown out by someone I bet,
I scooped it up, under my arm,
And headed home to work my charm.

'Please Mum, can we keep it, please,'
'But Katie, it's dirty and no doubt has fleas,'
'Can't we take it straight to the vet?'
'Well yes, we could and pay the large debt.'

'Listen Mum, she's purring, she likes our house,
And she'd catch that dreaded mouse,'
'Well I suppose she could stay,
But, she would have to keep out of the dog's way.'

Suddenly, the cat turned fierce,
And through my skin her claws did pierce,
She'd seen the dog and shook with fear,
Then chased after our dog so dear.

For days I had to separate the pair,
And just wished they'd learn to share,
After all, this was the dog's home,
The cat I rescued from having to roam.

I slowly showed her who was boss,
And that not behaving would be her loss,
But then one day I had a surprise,
I could hardly believe my eyes.

My dog and cat curled up together,
A sight I will remember forever.

Katie Peck (11)
The Robert Manning Technology College

POEM

Hamsters are cute and furry.
But watch out for when they get angry
Their bite's worse than you think.

Dogs are friendly when they want to be.
But watch out when they're playful
They can be quite boisterous you know.

With birds you have to be patient.
But if you train them every day
You will gain their trust in the end.

With ponies you also have to be patient.
But if you wait long enough
You will get a reward in the end.

Cats are quite tame.
But when they think they're in danger
They will scratch you.
So watch out!

Natalie Smith (11)
The Robert Manning Technology College

CHICKEN POX

Bored and grumpy
No fun company,
Nothing to do but scratch and itch
No fun this week on the football pitch,
Watching TV is no fun
When morning and night it's all you've done,
Spotty body, runny nose
Moaning at Mum about itchy bed clothes,
'Can my friends come round and play?'
'No, they don't want to take this disease away!'
Paint on the white stuff
To keep the itching at bay.
This I need to do most of the day,
I have found that there's no joy
In being a poorly boy
No jelly and ice-cream for me,
Mum gives me chicken soup and beef tea.
Chicken Pox is no fun
Scratch and itch, it's all I've done.

Thomas Wilson (11)
The Robert Manning Technology College

BMXING

B   MXing is the best if you like a test.
M   ountain bikes don't stand a chance.
X   treme sports it falls under.
I   ncredible air is needed to do good stunts.
N   early every time you fall off you hurt yourself.
G   etting on the bike is easy but pulling stunts is not.

Sean Burrell (12)
The Robert Manning Technology College

FOREST

In the middle of the forest
it's deep and dark

But in the darkest
light breaks through

The shadow's banished
good reigns

The bells of blue dances
in the green

Here I can stay
in my dream

Safe and warm in the
sun's gleam.

Chris Bains (13)
The Robert Manning Technology College

SCHOOL

School can be cool
School can be fun
School can be good
Good for everyone

School can be strict
School can be hard
School prefects stand on guard

School can be boring
School can be ace
School can fit a lot of people in one place.

Sam Ray (11)
The Robert Manning Technology College

MY HOLIDAY

We went away on holiday
We drove across to France
But there weren't any discos
So we couldn't dance.

The site was covered in tall fir trees
But the cones we couldn't reach
So we put on our bikinis
And walked down to the beach.

Down on the coastline
We didn't see any caves
Just lots and lots of seaweed
Bobbing in the waves.

Walking back along the beach
With my friends all hand-in-hand
Looking for shiny pebbles
Buried in the sand.

When you're walking in the sun
One thing we quickly learnt
If you didn't wear any sun cream
You could easily get burnt.

Nell Stubbs (11)
The Robert Manning Technology College